CW00866792

Ninja Penguin
Talks Japanese in Japan

Clay & Yumi Boutwell
with
CJ Martin

Copyright © 2013 Kotoba Books
www.KotobaInc.com
www.TheJapanShop.com

ISBN: 1484825470
ISBN-13: 978-1484825471

OTHER TITLES BY KOTOBA BOOKS
AVAILABLE IN EBOOK AND PAPERBACK

Hiragana, the Basics of Japanese
Japanese Reader Collection Vol 1: Hikoichi
Japanese Reader Collection Vol 2: Momotaro, the Peach Boy
Japanese Grammar 100 in Plain English
Kanji 100: Learn the Most Useful Kanji in Japanese
Kotowaza, Japanese Proverbs and Sayings

**A special thanks to Susan Glinert Stevens
for her excellent advice.**

INTRODUCTION

Penguin's dream of completing Ninja Academy has finally come true...

Almost.

One test remains: he must journey to the far frigid shores of Hokkaido in order to become a true Ninja Penguin. Besides, it is simply too hot in the sub-tropical Okinawa. Hokkaido, in northern Japan with its far more reasonable climate, sounds *REALLY* nice to a penguin who had been training many seasons in the Okinawan heat.

A penguin, as you know, is a flightless bird. Our hero, despite his extraordinary reflexes, is no different. He must, therefore, brave the long and arduous journey solely on webbed feet, defeating the many Ninja Masters who will test his knowledge along the way.

This book chronicles what the penguin experienced as he toured the forty-seven prefectures that make up Japan. He learned much about Japanese culture and geography while picking up more than 500 useful vocabulary words. You too can learn these important beginner-level words with the helpful hints and puzzles found throughout this book. As you work through each lesson, we invite you to listen to the especially formatted audio files. **You'll find the download link for the *free* MP3s on the last page.**

NOTE:

This book is a companion to the upcoming iPhone/iPad app, Ninja Penguin Learns Japanese in Japan. **If you would like to be notified when it is released, please email us:** <u>help@TheJapanShop.com</u>.

Please email us with any questions you may have. We want you to not only have success with your Japanese, but to enjoy your journey along the way!

ありがとうございます！

Clay & Yumi Boutwell
<u>www.TheJapanShop.com</u>
<u>help@theJapanShop.com</u>

&

CJ Martin
<u>www.CJMartinBooks.com</u>

CONTENTS

Contents

A Penguin Journey—a Memoir by Master Ninja Penguin

Penguins are not native to Okinawa. 当たり前！
Atari mae!—common sense, you might say, but you would be surprised how many humans are ignorant of even the most rudimentary facts of penguinology.

But our story begins shortly after I graduated from the Okinawan Ninjutsu Academy for Fowls under Master Namakemono, the revered sloth.

Yikes! It was hot there. And just to get it out before the uncomfortable question becomes inevitable: yes, I am a penguin.

A penguin who types, you ask?

Why, of course not, you knucklehead! Penguins can't type!

My three flabby fingers preclude any form of keyboard interaction. I simply dictate to my secretary, Mrs. Tsuru the Crane, and presto, she taps each letter with her long beak!

And, you there—wipe that snarky expression off your face. Just because I can't type doesn't mean I can't speak Japanese. Many humans don't realize it, but we penguins are exceptionally talented with language. I myself can speak half a dozen fluently; a bloke down ten or twenty rows in my flock can speak thirty-eight!

However, we never flaunt our superiority. If we did, National Geographic would be here in a flash taking some or all of us back to eager mad scientists waiting by their freaky instruments of torture...

But my super ninja-senses tell me that is not why you bought this book.

I, Master Ninja Penguin, will now recount my journey from Penguin to Ninja Penguin, from Okinawa to Hokkaido, translated for the first time from the original Penguinese.

I will only allow you to continue if you promise to not tip off National Geographic. If you do squeal, I simply warn you, I have a mean flipper chop.

With that singular stipulation agreed upon, let us begin...

Ninja Penguin began his journey in Okinawa...

忍者ペンギン

ninja penguin

1. Okinawa 沖縄

Japanese: 沖縄県 *okinawa ken*

Capital: 那覇 Naha

Population: 1,379,338 (December 1, 2008)

沖縄県
Symbol

Okinawa Prefecture

Kanji: 沖縄
Region: OKINAWA 沖縄

DID YOU KNOW?

"*Ken*" means prefecture. So, *okinawa-ken* means Okinawa Prefecture. There are 47 prefectures in Japan and this book will give a brief survey of each one. All of them, except a few metropolitan areas, use the designator *ken*.

Okinawa is a sub-tropical prefecture very different from the rest of Japan in culture, food, and even language.

Places to See:

- **Water**—beautiful white sand beaches, fishing, diving, whale watching, and other water related activities.
- **Yaeyama Islands**—Okinawa's southernmost island group, closer to Taiwan than even Okinawa's capital, Naha.
- **Yonaguni** (a part of the Yaeyama Island group) Beneath the waves, it is home to mysterious underwater ruins. It is a platform carved out of solid rock at perfectly right angles. How it was made and by whom is a mystery.
- **Shuri Castle**—the palace of the Ryuukyuu Kingdom.

Famous for:

- **Karate**—the martial art began in Okinawa.
- **Sugar cane, Pineapple** and **tropical fruits.**
- *Sanshin*—a three stringed instrument like a banjo.
- **Longevity**—Okinawans have the world's longest lifespan.
- **Shisa**—a traditional Ryukyuan decoration resembling a cross between a lion and a dog.
- Okinawa has its own language that is difficult for other Japanese speakers to understand.

Vocabulary Lesson 1: Colors

白 *shiro* white

紫 *murasaki* purple

緑 *midori* green

赤 *aka* red

茶色 *chairo* brown

黒 *kuro* black

灰色 *haiiro* gray

色 *iro* color

(LISTEN TO THE SOUND FILES FOR CORRECT PRONUNCIATION.)

As shown above, the word for "color" is *iro*. There are a few color names that incorporate *iro* in the word. These are usually named for something that is commonly found in that color. For example, *haiiro* (gray) actually means "the color of ashes" and *chairo* (brown) means "the color of tea."

Traffic signals in Japan are red (*aka*), yellow (*kiiro*), and... blue (*ao*)! The distinction of blue and green in Japanese can be a little fuzzy:

青信号 *ao shingou*—a green traffic light (literally, "blue light").

14

BATTLE ONE: Master Panda's Challenge.

Write your answers in romaji:
(The first one is done for you)

ACROSS

2 black
4 red
6 brown
8 gray

DOWN

1 purple
3 green
5 white
7 color

(ANSWERS IN THE BACK)

15

Notes from the Penguin #2

I spent many a day studying under Master Namakemono, the revered sloth. Training was grueling for many reasons: the long hours spent in the dojo, the constant taunting by the native "flying" birds, but must of all, the terrible heat.

I am a penguin. Hot weather and I never get along. Okinawa is the southernmost prefecture of Japan—nigh near the equator—the only prefecture that is truly subtropical. For those slow-witted human readers, that means it is hot!

I spent weeks traversing the many islands that make up the prefecture known as Okinawa and doing so, I made many acute observations. Okinawans are known for their longevity—the longest living people in the world. Add to that the fact that karate began in Okinawa and you have a pretty cool place—except that it is not cool at all...

Okinawa was simply too hot for my sensitive feathered skin. Upon graduation, I quickly swam my way to Kyushu in search of some relief.

TURN THE PAGE TO TRAVEL THE 473 MILES (761 KM)
TO KAGOSHIMA IN KYUSHU.

2. Kagoshima 鹿児島

Japanese: 鹿児島県 *kagoshima ken*
Capital: 鹿児島 Kagoshima
Population: 1,703,406 (December 1, 2010)

DID YOU KNOW?

Spanning some 600 kilometers from north to south, Kagoshima is the southernmost prefecture of the southernmost main island (not including Okinawa). Japan is made up of four main islands in addition to thousands of smaller ones. This region is called 九州 *kyuushuu*. In the old days, Kagoshima was a part of the Satsuma province that played a major role in the Meiji Restoration.

Places to See:

- **Sakurajima**—an active volcano near Kagoshima City.
- **Ibusuki**—hot spring resorts.
- **Lake Ikeda**—some say a monster similar to the Loch Ness called "Isshi" lives here.
- **The Flower Park Kagoshima**—the largest flower garden in Japan with 400,000 flowers and trees of 2,400 different species.

Famous for:

- **Saigo Takamori**—an influential samurai whose life inspired the 2003 movie, *The Last Samurai,* was born and died in Kagoshima.
- **Green tea**—the second largest producer next to Shizuoka.
- **Sweet potato.**
- **Unagi eels.**
- **Sakurajima daikon radish**—the largest radish in the world (pictured below).

Vocabulary Lesson 2: Basic Numbers

一 *ichi* one

二 *ni* two

三 *san* three

四 *shi*; *yon* four [two pronunciations]

五 *go* five

六 *roku* six

七 *shichi*; *nana* seven [two pronunciations]

八 *hachi* eight

九 *kyuu*; *ku* nine [two pronunciations]

十 *juu* ten

Counting in Japanese is a little more complicated than 1-2-3. There are actually two sets of numbers—at least for numbers up to ten: the **native Japanese** numbers called *kun-yomi* and those imported from **Chinese** many, many years ago called *on-yomi*.

The above are the *on-yomi* pronunciations. Learn them well. Knowing these ten words will allow you to count up to 99 and then learning three more words [**see page 171**], you can count up to 99,999,999!

3. Miyazaki 宮崎

Japanese: 宮崎県 *miyazaki ken*
Capital: 宮崎 Miyazaki
Population: 1,128,412 (December 1, 2010)

DID YOU KNOW?

Miyazaki is famous for a beautiful coastline facing the Pacific and for being the birthplace of the mythical first Japanese emperor, Emperor Jimmu.

Places to See:

- **The Nichinan Coastline**—a beautiful tropical paradise.
- **Aoshima Island**—a small island surrounded by rock formations that appear to be man-made, but are actually natural formations.
- **Kirishima**—a national park with volcanic mountains; Obi Castle Town—the main castle of the Ito clan during the Edo period (1603-1867)—mostly reconstructed, but much of the Edo period wall remains.
- **Takachiho Gorge**—a narrow gorge cut through dense rock by the Gokase River. The sheer cliffs, vegetation, and beautiful Minainotaki waterfall make the Takachiho Gorge a must for any nature/water lover.

Famous for:

- Surfing—in Hyuga.
- **Beautiful mountainous and coastal scenery.**
- **Mangos.**
- **Asahi Kasei**—a large Japanese chemical company is based in Nobeoka, Miyazaki.

Okinawa **Kyushu** Shikoku Chugoku Kansai Chubu Kanto Tohoku Hokkaido

Vocabulary Lesson 3: Basic Adjectives

暑い *atsui* hot (weather)

寒い *samui* cold (weather)

冷たい *tsumetai* cold (touch)

新しい *atarashii* new

古い *furui* old (not new)

早い *hayai* fast

遅い *osoi* slow

長い *nagai* long

短い *mijikai* short

難しい *muzukashii* difficult

簡単 *kantan* simple

There are two types of adjectives in Japanese: the *–i* adjectives and the *–na* adjectives. These are so named because all *–i* adjectives end with an *i* and all *–na* adjectives add a *na* when placed before nouns.

All of the above are *–i* adjectives except the last one which is a *–na* adjective. It was added to contrast *muzukashii*.

22

Battle Two: MASTER NEKO'S CHALLENGE

ACROSS

2 five
4 difficult
5 long
7 short
9 cold (weather)
10 fast
13 old
16 one
17 eight

DOWN

1 cold (to the touch)
3 slow
5 two
6 new
8 simple
11 hot (weather)
12 ten
14 six
15 three

4. Kumamoto 熊本

Japanese: 熊本県 *kumamoto ken*
Capital: 熊本 Kumamoto
Population: 1,812,255 (May 1, 2011)

DID YOU KNOW?

The origin of the bear... that is what Kumamoto means. Kumamoto is at the heart of Kyushu.

Places to See:

- **Kumamoto Castle**—built in 1467, expanded in 1601, destroyed in 1877, rebuilt in the 1960s.
- **Mt. Asa**—one of the world's largest active volcanoes!
- **Suizen-ji Jōjuen**—a Japanese garden originally constructed in 1636 as a tea retreat for a lord. It features an artificial mountain in the shape of Mt. Fuji.
- **Tsūjun Bridge**—the largest stone aqueduct in Japan. It was built in 1854.

Famous for:

- **Hot springs.**
- **Mount Aso**—a large active volcano.
- The iconic **Kumamoto Castle.**
- **Basashi**—raw horse meat.

Okinawa **Kyushu** Shikoku Chugoku Kansai Chubu Kanto Tohoku Hokkaido

Vocabulary Lesson 4: Getting Around

バス *basu* bus

タクシー *takushi-* taxi

電車 *densha* train

自転車 *jitensha* bicycle

駅 *eki* train station

車 *kuruma* car

切符 *kippu* ticket

地図 *chizu* map

歩く *aruku* to walk

飛行機 *hikouki* plane

船 *fune* boat/ship

電車 *densha* is a train powered by electricity. 汽車 *kisha*— now non-existent except for tourist rides—is a train powered by steam.

The heart of most Japanese cities is its train station, the 駅 *eki*. Japan has an amazingly well-developed and easy-to-access train system. You can get to just about any city or town by train.

Okinawa **Kyushu** Shikoku Chugoku Kansai Chubu Kanto Tohoku Hokkaido

5. Nagasaki 長崎

Japanese: 長崎県 *nagasaki ken*
Capital: 長崎 Nagasaki
Population: 1,407,904 (2012)

DID YOU KNOW?

Other than a sharing a short border with Saga Prefecture, there's plenty of water to go diving and other water activities.

Places to See:

- **Nagasaki Penguin Aquarium**—of course, this tops the list!
- **Inasayama**—from the top of this mountain, you can view 360 degrees of Nagasaki and its harbor. Beautiful at night.
- **Oura Catholic Church**—built in 1864 by French missionaries, it is the oldest standing church in Japan.
- **Atomic Bomb Museum & the Peace Park.**
- **Huis Ten Bosch**—a theme park that recreates the Netherlands with full-size copies of old Dutch buildings. The name means "House in the Forest."

Famous for:

- **Thomas Blake Glover**—a Scottish merchant who made Nagasaki his home, built the first western-style house in Japan, and was instrumental in helping Japan industrialize during the Meiji period.
- Nagasaki was the second city to have an **atomic bomb** dropped on it.
- **Dejima**—for two centuries this man-made island in the bay of Nagasaki was the only place Portuguese and Dutch traders could port. Land reclamation projects have since surrounded it with streets and modern buildings.
- Nagasaki is the setting of Puccini's opera, *Madama Butterfly*.

Okinawa **Kyushu** Shikoku Chugoku Kansai Chubu Kanto Tohoku Hokkaido

- **Meganebashi**—"eyeglass bridge" is the grandest of several ancient stone bridges that cross the Nakajima river. This bridge was constructed in 1634.

 Vocabulary Lesson 5: Directions

上 *ue* up
下 *shita* down
左 *hidari* left
右 *migi* right
前 *mae* front
後ろ *ushiro* behind
東 *higashi* east
西 *nishi* west
南 *minami* south
北 *kita* north

You may recognize the kanji for "east" 東 *higashi* in Tokyo 東京 *toukyou*. This is because Tokyo means "east capital."

Nearly all kanji have at least two readings. In this case, 東 can be pronounced *higashi* or *tou*. The first, *higashi*, is the native Japanese pronunciation, or *kun* reading. *Tou* is the Chinese or *on* reading.

In general, when a kanji character is paired with another kanji, you use the *on* reading as in *toukyou*.

Battle Three: MASTER KUMA'S CHALLENGE

Okinawa **Kyushu** Shikoku Chugoku Kansai Chubu Kanto Tohoku Hokkaido

ACROSS

3 boat/ship
6 taxi
8 east
10 train
13 to walk
16 ticket
17 map
18 south
20 north
21 west

DOWN

1 up
2 bicycle
4 behind
5 right
7 left
9 bus
11 train station
12 plane
14 car
15 down
19 front

6. Saga 佐賀

Japanese: 佐賀県 *saga ken*
Capital: 佐賀 Saga
Population: 858,603 (February 1, 2008)

DID YOU KNOW?

Kyushu's smallest prefecture hosts a major annual hot air balloon festival. Alas, official rules forbid flightless birds from participating.

Places to See:

- **Ogi Park**—one of the best places in Japan to see cherry blossoms.
- **Yoshinogari Site**—a large Yayoi archaeological site with ruins dating back 2,000 years. Ancient structures have been reconstructed making Yoshinogari an interesting place to visit.

Famous for:

- **Ceramics and Porcelain**—Arita-yaki, Imari-yaki, and Karatsu-yaki are highly prised porcelain from the area.
- **Saga Balloon Fiesta**—every November, millions of spectators come to see hundreds of huge hot air balloons fly.
- **Surfing and Skiing.**
- **Yutoku Inari Shrine**—one of Japan's three largest Inari shrines.
- **Mochigome**—Saga is Japan's largest producer of *mochigome*, sticky rice used in special foods such as *mochi*, the traditional rice cake made on New Year's Day.

Vocabulary Lesson 6: Which One?

大きい *ookii* big

小さい *chiisai* small

一番 *ichiban* #1; the best

高い *takai* high (price or spatial height)

安い *yasui* cheap

低い *hikui* low

思い *omoi* heavy

軽い *karui* light (weight)

たくさん *takusan* many

少ない *sukunai* few

少し *sukoshi* a little

A building can be *takai*. So can the price of something. To say someone is tall, you need to say "one's statue is tall":

背が高い *se ga takai*—tall (a person's height)

Likewise, to say someone is short:

背が低い *se ga hikui*—short (a person's height)

And here is a phrase that may be useful for you now:

日本語が少し話せます。
nihongo ga sukoshi hanasemasu.
(I) can speak Japanese a little.

Okinawa **Kyushu** Shikoku Chugoku Kansai Chubu Kanto Tohoku Hokkaido

7. Fukuoka 福岡

Japanese: 福岡県 *fukuoka ken*
Capital: 福岡 Fukuoka
Population: 5,071,732 (September 1, 2010)

DID YOU KNOW?

Fukuoka is the largest prefecture in Kyushu and Fukuoka City is the most populated. Fukuoka is closer to Shanghai and Seoul than Tokyo.

Places to See:

- **Fukuoka Tower**—a 234 meters (768 feet) high iconic symbol of Fukuoka.
- **The Ruins of Fukuoka Castle**—this was the largest castle in Kyushu in the Edo period (1603-1867) but was intentionally destroyed during the Meiji Restoration due to its symbolic past.
- **Canal City Hakata**—a large shopping mall with hundreds of shops, restaurants, and game centers.

Famous for:

- **Gion Yamakasa**—Every July, racers push beautifully decorated festival floats five kilometers.
- **Yatai**—food stalls famous for ramen.
- Produces **automobiles, semiconductors, and steel.**
- **Bridgestone Tires and Best Denki** electronics chain were founded in Fukuoka.
- **Ramen**—Fukuoka is famous for the many ramen food stalls that pop up after dark.
- **Hakata Dontaku Festival**—Japan's largest citizen's annual festival, which started in 1179!

Okinawa **Kyushu** Shikoku Chugoku Kansai Chubu Kanto Tohoku Hokkaido

Vocabulary Lesson 7: Pronouns

私 *watashi* I; me

あなた *anata* you (singular)

私たち *watashi tachi* we; us

あなたたち *anata tachi* you (plural)

彼 *kare* he; him

彼女 *kanojo* she; her

彼ら *karera* they; them

ぼく *boku* me (used by males)

君 *kimi* you (used by males)

Japanese has an extraordinary large number or pronouns—especially for the first and second person. For example, to say I or me, you can use: *watashi, watakushi, boku, ore, washi, waga, sessha, ware, uchi,* and others with varying usefulness and politeness.

However, **pronouns are only rarely used.** If the context is clear, you don't have to repeat the subject.

お名前は？
onamae wa?
(What is your) name?

青木です。
aoki desu.
(I) am Aoki.

36

Battle Four: MASTER TANUKI'S CHALLENGE

ACROSS

4 you (plural)
8 we; us
9 me (used by males)

DOWN

1 you (singular)
2 they; them
3 I; me
5 you (used by males)
6 she; her
7 he; him

Okinawa **Kyushu** Shikoku Chugoku Kansai Chubu Kanto Tohoku Hokkaido

8. Oita 大分

Japanese: 大分県 *ooita ken*
Capital: 大分 Ooita
Population: 1,209,587 (October 1, 2005)

DID YOU KNOW?

If you like the Japanese Onsen—hot springs—you will love the rural Oita prefecture.

Places to See:

- **Shouen Village**—the landscape and rice fields have been kept intact for 800 years.
- **Harajiri Falls**—one of Japan's top waterfalls.
- **Beppu**—capital city for hot springs with eight major geothermal hot spots.
- **Kuju Mountains**—volcanic mountain range that is a part of the Aso-Kuju National Park.

Famous for:

- **Onsen**—many hot springs.
- **Yufuin Onsen**—a hot springs town with approximately four million visitors a year.

Vocabulary Lesson 8: Houses

家 *ie* house
階 *kai* floor of a building
ビル *biru* building
アパート *apaato* apartment
部屋 *heya* room
居間 *ima* living room
トイレ *toire* bathroom; a toilet
玄関 *genkan* entrance
台所 *daidokoro* kitchen
お風呂 *ofuro* bath/bathroom

A large apartment is called a マンション *manshon* in Japanese. While it comes from the English word "mansion," a Japanese マンション just means a luxurious apartment or condominium.

If you want to use a more Japanese sounding word for "bathroom," you can say お手洗い *ote arai* which literally means "(the place) to wash one's hands."

The 玄関 *genkan* is a special place at the entrance of all homes and most buildings where people entering remove their shoes and put on slippers or inside shoes. It is a breach of etiquette to enter a house with outside shoes on.

9. Ehime 愛媛

Japanese: 愛媛県 *ehime ken*
Capital: 松山 Matsuyama
Population: 1,430,086 (November 1, 2010)

DID YOU KNOW?

Shikoku (四国), literally, "four kingdoms," is so named because the large island houses four prefectures.

Ehime (愛媛) means "the love princess."

Places to See:

- **Dogo Onsen**, Japan's oldest hot spring—over 1,300 years of history!
- **Matsuyama Castle**—originally built in 1603, modern restoration work began in 1966.

 Famous for:

- **Shipbuilding**—biggest in Japan.
- **Haiku** originated in Ehime.
- **Mikan** oranges.
- **Bamboo Craft.**
- **Botchan**—Natsume Soseki's novel, Botchan, is set in Matsuyama, Ehime.

愛媛

Vocabulary Lesson 9: Demonstrative Pronouns

これ *kore* this thing [replaces a noun]

それ *sore* that thing (near listener)

あれ *are* that thing (far away)

どれ *dore* which thing?

この *kono* this [used with a noun]

その *sono* that (near listener)

あの *ano* that (far away)

どの *dono* which

ここ *koko* here

そこ *soko* there (near listener)

あそこ *asoko* there (far away)

どこ *doko* where

Demonstrative pronouns and their cousins are demonstratively difficult for English speakers. But they aren't too bad once you understand that there are three categories of usage:

1. Near to the speaker
2. Near to the listener
3. Away from either speaker or listener

See **Appendix C** for a full list of these important *Ko-so-a-do* words.

Okinawa Kyushu **Shikoku** Chugoku Kansai Chubu Kanto Tohoku Hokkaido

Battle Five: MASTER INU'S CHALLENGE

ACROSS

2 here
3 that (near listener)
4 that (far away)
6 which
7 which thing?
8 there (near listener)
9 that thing (near listener)

DOWN

1 there (far away)
2 this [used with a noun]
4 that thing (far away)
5 this thing [replaces a noun]
7 where

Okinawa Kyushu Shikoku Chugoku Kansai Chubu Kanto Tohoku Hokkaido

10. Kochi 高知

Japanese: 高知県 *kōchi ken*
Capital: 高知 Kōchi
Population: 757,914 (December 1, 2011)

DID YOU KNOW?

The largest, but least populous prefecture in the Shikoku region, Kochi is famous for its many rivers.

Places to See:

- **Inamura Mountain**—the highest mountain in Kochi.
- **Kochi Castle**—one of twelve original castles still standing in Japan. There are many reconstructed castles, but most were torn down during the Meiji Restoration or destroyed by fire or war. Kochi Castle was constructed in 1611 and most of the buildings standing are originals.
- **Anpanman Museum**—beloved by Japanese children everywhere, the bread-faced Anpanman has his own museum in Kochi.
- **Makino Park**—famous for its cherry blossoms.

Famous for:

- The bread-faced comic hero **Anpanman** originated in Kochi.
- **Katsuo no tataki**—seasoned bonito tuna.
- **Yosakoi festival**—a three day matsuri with thousands of dancers in colorful costumes.
- Birthplace of the Meiji reformer, **Ryoma Sakamoto** and **Yanase Takashi**, the creator of Anpanman.
- **Shimanto River**—the longest river in Shikoku is located in western Kochi and away from major cities, preserving clear, clean water.

Vocabulary Lesson 10: Being Polite

ありがとうございます *arigatou gozaimasu* Thank you.

いらっしゃいませ *irasshaimase* Welcome! (to customers)

はじめまして *hajimemashite* Nice to meet you.

おはようございます *ohayou gozaimasu* Good morning.

今日は *konnichi wa* Good afternoon.

今晩は *konban wa* Good evening.

お休みなさい *oyasumi nasai* Good night.

すみません *sumimasen* Excuse me.

失礼します *shitsureishimasu* I am being rude.

どうぞ *douzo* please; help yourself

いただきます *itadakimasu* I receive (before eating).

Being polite in Japanese is far more important than it usually is in English. Before opening your mouth, you have to consider the social level of (or your relationship with) the person you are speaking to. Generally, use more polite language with those older than you, people you have just met, and those in authority over you.

It is a good rule to always suffix other people's names with –*san*. Even with people you consider friends, use –*san* until they ask you not to.

Never, ever, refer to yourself with –*san*.

11.   Tokushima 徳島

Japanese: 徳島県 *tokushima ken*
Capital: 徳島 Tokushima
Population: 824,108 (October 1, 2001)

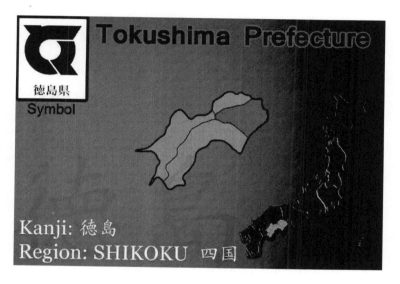

DID YOU KNOW?

The Tokushima symbol is a stylized melding of the hiragana
と *to* and く *ku* making the first two characters for
TOKUshima.

Places to See:

- **Ichinomiya Castle and Tokushima Castle** ruins.
- **Omotegoten Garden**—near Tokushima Castle Museum.
- **Mt. Bizan**—the symbol of Tokushima City. The whole of Tokushima City can be seen from its top.

Famous for:

- **Produce**—Naruto sweet potatoes, sudachi citrus fruit, lotus roots, and strawberries.
- **Awa-odori Dance Festival**—held every August featuring shamisen (traditional three-stringed instrument), drums, and traditional dance.
- **Naruto Whirlpools**—large whirlpools in the Naruto Straits between the main Shikoku island and Awaji Island.
- **Kazurabashi**—bridges made from mountain vines.

Vocabulary Lesson 11: Basic Body Parts

体 *karada* body
頭 *atama* head
指 *yubi* finger
首 *kubi* neck
手 *te* hand
肩 *kata* shoulder
足 *ashi* leg/foot
肘 *hiji* elbow
膝 *hiza* knee
腕 *ude* arm
おなか *onaka* stomach

Sometimes, Japanese is very clever when combining words. For example, your wrist isn't a special word. It is just the "neck of the hand": 手首 *te kubi*. Your ankle is 足首 *ashi kubi* (the neck of the leg).

Children riding on shoulders are doing 肩車 *kata guruma* [*kata*—shoulder + *kuruma*—car/vehicle (with a sound change)]. If you play thumb wrestling, you are playing 指相撲 *yubi zumou* [*yubi*—finger + *sumou*—sumo (with a sound change)].

Battle Six: MASTER TANUKI'S CHALLENGE

JAPAN IS MADE UP OF FOUR MAIN ISLANDS, BUT THOUSANDS OF SMALLER ISLANDS.

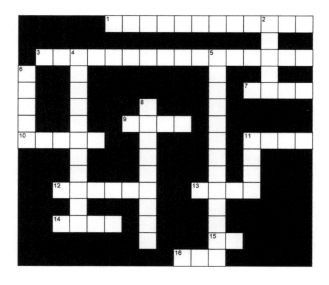

ACROSS

1 Welcome (to customers).
3 I am being rude.
7 shoulder
9 neck
10 stomach
11 knee
12 body
13 leg/foot
14 finger
15 hand
16 arm

DOWN

2 head
4 I receive (before eating).
5 Nice to meet you.
6 please; help yourself
8 Excuse me.
11 elbow

Okinawa Kyushu Shikoku Chugoku Kansai Chubu Kanto Tohoku Hokkaido

12.   Kagawa 香川

Japanese: 香川県 *kagawa ken*
Capital: 高松 Takamatsu
Population: 995,465 (December 1, 2010)

DID YOU KNOW?

Kagawa is the smallest prefecture in area in Japan.

Places to See:

- **Yashima**—a mountain battlefield for a major battle between the Heike and Genji clans on March 22, 1185.
- **Ritsurin Garden**—established in 1625, Ritsurin Garden became a prefectural garden open to the public in 1875.
- **Marugame Castle**—originally built in 1597, today, stone walls, two gates, and the keep remain.
- **Takamatsu Castle**—completed in 1590, it is one of only three castles in Japan with water moats.
- **Kotohiki Park**—in Kanonji City, Kotohiki Park is famous for its cherry blossoms.

Famous for:

- **Sanuki Udon**—a noodle soup made with tuna and kelp.
- **Great Seto Bridge**—the world's longest two-tiered bridge system. It connects Shikoku with the main island, Honshu. It has two lanes of highway traffic in each direction, and a railway track in the lower deck.
- **Konpirasan**—a shrine remarkable in that it incorporates both Shinto and Buddhist elements.

Vocabulary Lesson 12: Counting Things

一つ *hitotsu* one thing
二つ *futatsu* two things
三つ *mittsu* three things
四つ *yottsu* four things
五つ *itsutsu* five things
六つ *muttsu* six things
七つ *nanatsu* seven things
八つ *yattsu* eight things
九つ *kokonotsu* nine things
十 *too* ten things

Japanese has two systems for counting. For up to ten, both the "Chinese" and "Japanese" ways are used. The above are the ten native Japanese words and are used mainly for counting general objects and the days of the month.

In addition, Japanese has what are called "counters" added to numbers when counting most things. In English, you say, "One cup of coffee" instead of "one coffee." Counters in Japanese work similarly. The most common counters are *ko* (for counting most small objects), *hon* (for counting long, slender objects), and *hiki* or *piki* (for counting most animals).

Please see **Appendix B** for a fuller discussion on counting in Japanese.

We took some liberties with this comic. First off, penguins only have three "fingers" and there seems to be some dispute as to whether one of them should be considered a thumb. Next, hitchhiking isn't common in Japan, although some people (mostly foreigners) do it. Lastly, the "bird" isn't an offensive gesture in Japan, but most people do know it is offensive in Western culture having seen it in countless American movies.

13. Yamaguchi 山口

Japanese: 山口県 *yamaguchi ken*
Capital: 山口 Yamaguchi
Population: 1,445,702 (May 1, 2011)

DID YOU KNOW?

Yamaguchi is one of the few prefectures whose largest city, Shimonoseki, isn't the capital (Yamaguchi City).

The Chōshū Domain (長州藩 *chōshū han*) during the Edo Period was in the Yamaguchi area.

The underwater Kanmon Tunnel connects Yamaguchi to Kyushu.

Places to See:

- **Kintai Bridge**—built in 1673, this bridge spans the Nishiki River in a series of five arches. This wooden bridge is considered a symbol of Western Honshu.

- **Kikko Park** and **Tokiwa Park**.
- **Hagi Castle ruins**—built in 1604 and destroyed during the Meiji Restoration.

Famous for:

- **Fugu**—pufferfish, the only food the Emperor of Japan is forbidden to eat due to it being poisonous.
- **Akiyoshidai Quasi-national Park**—has Japan's longest cave, the Akiyoshido.
- Yamaguchi City is known as "**the Kyoto of the West**" for emulating the city planning of Kyoto.

Vocabulary Lesson 13: -na Adjectives

有名な *yuumei na* famous
変な *hen na* strange
上手な *jouzu na* skilled
下手な *heta na* unskilled
便利な *benri na* convenient
不便な *fuben na* inconvenient
好きな *suki na* likable
大事な *daiji na* important
元気な *genki na* energetic; healthy
静かな *shizuka na* quiet

These are all –na adjectives, so called because they require a "*na*" added when placed before nouns. Without a noun, you don't need a "*na*."

静か *shizuka*—quiet
静かな夜 *shizuka na yoru*—a quiet night

有名 *yuumei*—famous
有名な人 *yuumei na hito*—a famous person

元気 *genki*—healthy; energetic
元気な子 *genki na ko*—an energetic child

14.   Hiroshima 広島

Japanese: 広島県 *hiroshima ken*
Capital: 広島 Hiroshima
Population: 2,857,990 (March 1, 2011)

DID YOU KNOW?

Hiroshima is, of course, best known for the atomic bombing that ended World War II, but it is worth a visit for many other reasons including the iconic Miyajima Torii and who can miss seeing the world's largest wooden rice scoop!

Places to See:

- **The Atomic Dome**—the only structure left standing near the bomb's hypocenter.
- **Hiroshima Peace Memorial Park.**
- **The Itsukushima Shrine**—including the iconic "floating" *torii* gate, Miyajima Torii. It appears to float in the bay.
- **Oshakushi**—the world's largest wooden rice scoop which is 7.7 meters long (25 feet)!
- **Takehara**—Edo Period merchant houses.

Famous for:

- One of only two cities to have had an **atomic bomb** dropped on it.
- **Mazda's headquarters.**
- **Shipbuilding.**
- The many **ancient Japanese and Chinese styled shrines and temples.**
- **Okonomiyaki**—Japanese pancake grilled with various ingredients such as egg, cabbage, and meat.
- **Hiroshima Carp**—Hiroshima's professional baseball team based at Mazda Stadium.

Okinawa Kyushu Shikoku **Chugoku** Kansai Chubu Kanto Tohoku Hokkaido

Okinawa Kyushu Shikoku **Chugoku** Kansai Chubu Kanto Tohoku Hokkaido

 Vocabulary Lesson 14: Question Words

何 *nani/nan* what? [two pronunciations]
誰 *dare* who?
いつ *itsu* when?
どちら *dochira* which one?
どう *dou* how?
なぜ *naze* why?
いくら *ikura* how much?
どうやって *douyatte* how to do?
いくつ *ikutsu* how many?
何時 *nanji* what time?

何 can either be *nani* or *nan*. Usually when by itself, you use *nani*. When added to something else, use *nan*.

これは何？
kore wa nani?
What is this?

何時ですか？
nanji desu ka?
What time is it?

何 *nan* when added to something shows uncertainty. Let's look at a few ways it is used as a counter.

何人 ***nan nin*** how many people	くるのは何人^{なんにん}ですか？ *kuru no wa nan nin desu ka?* How many people are coming?
何年 ***nan nen*** how many years	何年^{なんねん}アメリカに住^すんでいましたか？ *nan nen amerika ni sunde imashita ka?* How many years did you live in America?
何番 ***nan ban*** what number	次^{つぎ}は何番^{なんばん}ですか？ *tsugi wa nan ban desu ka?* What is the next number?
何個 ***nan ko*** how many pieces	ジェリービーンを何個^{なんこ}ほしいですか？ *jeri-bi-n o nanko hoshii desu ka?* How many jelly beans do you want?

Battle Seven: MASTER INU'S CHALLENGE

ACROSS

2 quiet
5 what time?
7 unskilled
8 convenient
12 likable
15 skilled
16 important
17 energetic

DOWN

1 famous
3 strange
4 why?
6 how much?
9 how many?
10 which one?
11 inconvenient
13 when?
14 who?

15.   Shimane 島根

Japanese: 島根県 *shimane ken*
Capital: 松江 Matsue
Population: 712,336 (October 11, 2011)

DID YOU KNOW?

Shimane is the second least populous prefecture in Japan (Tottori ranks #1). But to make up for this embarrassment, Matsue, the capital, takes #1 as having the smallest population out of all the 47 prefectural capitals.

Okinawa Kyushu Shikoku **Chugoku** Kansai Chubu Kanto Tohoku Hokkaido

Places to See:

- **Iwami Ginzan Silver Mine**—a World Heritage site and, at one point, supplier of a third of the world's silver in the 17th century.
- The **Lafcadio Hearn Memorial Museum**, honoring the author of *Kwaidan* and other works showcasing Japan to the 19th century Western World.
- **Matsue Castle**—the second largest castle in Japan. Today, only the keep and some walls remain.
- **Hii River Bank** with over 800 trees is famous for viewing cherry blossoms.
- **Adachi Museum of Art**—in Yasugi, Shimane, this museum houses many works of modern Japanese art.

Famous for:

- In 1890 **Lafcadio Hearn** came to Shimane as an English teacher. His most famous work is *Kwaidan*, chronicling famous Japanese folk and ghost stories.
- **Izumo Soba Noodles.**
- **Akaten**—a local fish specialty.
- **Izumo Taisha**—Japan's oldest shrine.
- **Lake Shinji**—the seventh largest lake in Japan.

Vocabulary Lesson 15: Teen Numbers

十一 *juu ichi* eleven
十二 *juu ni* twelve
十三 *juu san* thirteen
十四 *juu yon* fourteen [also: *juu shi*]
十五 *juu go* fifteen
十六 *juu roku* sixteen
十七 *juu nana* seventeen [also: *juu shichi*]
十八 *juu hachi* eighteen
十九 *juu kyuu* nineteen [also: *juu ku*]
二十 *ni juu* twenty

Once you are beyond ten, just use the "Chinese" (*ichi, ni, san*) pronunciations—for the most part. There are a few special words for special topics, like 二十歳 *hatachi* for age twenty.

Please see **Appendix B** for more on counting in Japan.

Okinawa Kyushu Shikoku **Chugoku** Kansai Chubu Kanto Tohoku Hokkaido

16.   Okayama 岡山

Japanese: 岡山県 *okayama ken*
Capital: 岡山 Okayama
Population: 1,940,411 (January 1, 2012)

DID YOU KNOW?

The hometown of Momotaro, the Peach Boy. Also! Miyamoto Musashi, the world's greatest 17th century samurai, was from this area.

Places to See:

- **Korakuen**—one of the Three Great Gardens of Japan.
- **Okayama Castle**—also known as the "Crow Castle" due to its stark black paint.
- **Japanese Folk Toy Museum**—wide range of folk toys made throughout Japan from the 18th to 20th century.
- **Momotaro Karakuri Museum**—all you need to know about the Peach Boy.
- **Mimasaka**—the birthplace of the famous samurai Musashi Miyamoto.
- **Bitchu Matsuyama Castle**—one of the few remaining original castles in Japan. It is also the castle with the highest elevation above sea level in Japan.

Famous for:

- **Bizen-yaki**—Bizen pottery.
- Associated with the **Momotaro** legend—the most Japanese folk tale about a boy born from a peach.
- **Korakuen**—one of the Three Great Gardens of Japan
- **Textiles**—over half of the school uniforms in Japan are produced in Okayama.
- **Kibi Dango**—a famous sweet made from rice flour that originated in Okayama and is featured in the famous Momotaro traditional folktale.

Okinawa Kyushu Shikoku **Chugoku** Kansai Chubu Kanto Tohoku Hokkaido

Okinawa Kyushu Shikoku **Chugoku** Kansai Chubu Kanto Tohoku Hokkaido

 ## Vocabulary Lesson 16: Nature

山 *yama* mountain

川 *kawa* river

湖 *mizuumi* lake

海 *umi* sea

島 *shima* island

空 *sora* sky

林 *hayashi* woods

太陽 *taiyou* sun

月 *tsuki* moon

星 *hoshi* star

Notice the progression of the kanji for tree, woods, and forest.

木 *ki*—tree
林 *hayashi*—woods
森 *mori*—forest

Sometimes, discovering kanji relationships can help with recognition and memorization.

17. Tottori 鳥取

Japanese: 鳥取県 *tottori ken*
Capital: 鳥取 Tottori
Population: 584,982 (April 1, 2011)

DID YOU KNOW?

The symbol is a stylized hiragana と *to* shaped to look like a flying bird. The name 鳥取 *tottori* has the kanji, "bird" and "to take." It is also the least populous prefecture in Japan.

Okinawa Kyushu Shikoku **Chugoku** Kansai Chubu Kanto Tohoku Hokkaido

Places to See:

- **Tottori Castle ruins**—originally built around 1555, this mountain castle is now in ruins.
- **Tottori Sand Dunes**—the only large sand dune system in Japan. The name in Japanese is 鳥取砂丘 *tottori sakyuu.*
- **Kyusho Park and Utsubuki Park**—famous for the cherry blossoms.

Famous for:

- Agricultural products such as **nashi pear, nagaimo yam, negi onion, and the watermelon.**
- Major producer of **rice.**
- **Sand dunes.**
- **Hang gliding, paragliding, and sandboarding.**
- **Mount Daisen**—the tallest mountain in Western Japan.

Vocabulary Lesson 17: Japanese Animals

猫 *neko* cat

犬 *inu* dog

牛 *ushi* cow

熊 *kuma* bear

兎 *usagi* rabbit

狐 *kitsune* fox

猿 *saru* monkey

狼 *ookami* wolf

狸 *tanuki* tanuki (Japanese raccoon)

猪 *inoshishi* wild boar

Notice 猫 *neko* (cat), 狐 *kitsune* (fox), 猿 *saru* (monkey), 狼 *ookami* (wolf), 狸 *tanuki* (raccoon), and 猪 *inoshishi* (wild boar) all have the same kanji part to the left. This is common to wild animals.

Knowing the kanji parts can help you guess the meaning or sometimes pronunciation for even unknown kanji.

Battle Eight: MASTER TANUKI'S CHALLENGE

Visit www.Kotobainc.com for information on our apps.

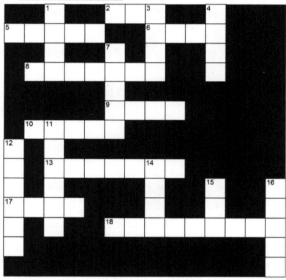

ACROSS

2 dog
5 rabbit
6 sky
8 forest
9 bear
10 star
13 fox
17 mountain
18 wild boar

DOWN

1 river
3 cow
4 monkey
7 moon
11 wolf
12 sun
14 cat
15 sea
16 island

Okinawa Kyushu Shikoku Chugoku Kansai Chubu Kanto Tohoku Hokkaido

18. Hyogo 兵庫

Japanese: 兵庫県 *Hyōgo ken*
Capital: 神戸 Kobe
Population: 5,582,978 (November 1, 2011)

DID YOU KNOW?

Hyogo prefecture borders two seas: the Sea of Japan to the north and the Inland Sea to the south. In 1180, the emperor moved the imperial court to what is now the city of Kobe, but for only five months!

Places to See:

- **Himeji Castle**—built with traditional wooden architecture and stone walls. Originally built in 1333 and expanded through the years, Himeji Castle remains intact even through typhoons, earthquakes, and bombings. It is one of the very few Japanese castles that is not a reconstruction.
- **Kinosaki Onsen**—this old-fashioned onsen town has been well known for its hot springs since the 8th century.
- **Kobe**—historic port for foreign trade in the 19th century that has gardens, shopping, museums, and the Kobe Port Tower with an observation deck.
- **Kitano Ijinkan**—a historical district containing Meiji-era foreign residences.

Famous for:

- **Metal and medical industries.**
- The World Heritage Site, **Himeji Castle.**
- The **1995 magnitude 7.2 Great Hanshin earthquake** which destroyed major parts of Kobe and killed 6,500 people.
- **Takarazuka**—famous for the all-female Broadway-esque theater productions.
- **Kobe beef**—beef from the Wagyu cattle raised according to tradition in Hyogo.

Okinawa Kyushu Shikoku Chugoku **Kansai** Chubu Kanto Tohoku Hokkaido

Vocabulary Lesson 18: Head Parts

顔 *kao* face
口 *kuchi* mouth
唇 *kuchibiru* lips
目 *me* eye
耳 *mimi* ear
顎 *ago* chin
舌 *shita* tongue
歯 *ha* tooth
鼻 *hana* nose
ほっぺ *hoppe* cheek
髪の毛 *kami no ke* hair (head)

More complex kanji usually have parts that hint at their meaning or pronunciation. For example, 聞く *kiku* (to ask; to listen) and 聴く *kiku* (also means "to listen" but with more intensity) both have 耳 *mimi* (ear) in them.

Another example is 言う *iu* (to speak), 語 *go* (language), and 歌う *utau* (to sing) all have 口 *kuchi* (mouth) in there and relate to sound.

Okinawa Kyushu Shikoku Chugoku **Kansai** Chubu Kanto Tohoku Hokkaido

Sumo is the national sport of Japan and Japan is the only country where it is practiced professionally. The sumo wrestlers have to order their lives strictly to ancient traditions.

A bout is won when the other wrestler is forced out of the ring or touches the ground with any body part other than the bottom of his feet.

A ukiyoe woodblock print by Utagawa Kunisada (1786-1865)

19.   Osaka 大阪

Japanese: 大阪府 *oosaka fu*
Capital: 大阪市 Osaka City
Population: 8,864,228 (January 1, 2012)

DID YOU KNOW?

Osaka is the first prefecture we've encountered not called "*ken*" (prefecture), but "*fu*" which is used for metropolitan prefectures. The first conveyor belt sushi restaurant—a regular feature found in all Japanese cities—originated in Higashiosaka in Osaka Prefecture.

Places to See:

- **Osaka Castle**—Osaka's most famous landmark. A reconstruction, but a very large castle.
- **Universal Studios Japan**—containing many of the same rides as the Universal Orlando Resort.
- **Osaka Aquarium**—one of the largest aquariums in the world.
- **Umeda Sky Building**—a skyscraper with an observation deck.
- **Mino Park**—one of the best places to see the autumn's colorful foliage.

Famous for:

- Electronic giants such as **Panasonic** and **Sharp**.
- **Shitennoji Temple**—established in 593 AD, Shitennoji is a large temple with a five story pagoda.
- Being **the opposite of Tokyo**: people stand to the right on escalators instead of left like in Tokyo; people from Osaka are bubbly and business-conscious. They may be seen as tight with their money. Tokyoites, on the other hand may be seen as cold, busy, and overstressed. Comedians come from Kansai. News reporters are from Tokyo.
- **Oosaka Zouheikyoku**—the Japanese mint producing coins and medals is located in Osaka.
- **Okonomi-yaki and Tako-yaki**—festival foods.

Okinawa Kyushu Shikoku Chugoku **Kansai** Chubu Kanto Tohoku Hokkaido

Vocabulary Lesson 19: Animals

キリン *kirin* giraffe

象 *zou* elephant

コアラ *koara* koala

カンガルー *kangaru-* kangaroo

ライオン *raion* lion

パンダ *panda* panda

馬 *uma* horse

豚 *buta* pig

羊 *hitsuji* sheep

虎 *tora* tiger

ネズミ *nezumi* mouse

山羊 *yagi* goat

For the most part, saying the name for a baby animal is as easy as adding 子 *ko* before the name of the animal:

> 子犬 *ko inu*—puppy
> [It is also sometimes written as 仔犬 and 小犬.]
> 子猫 *ko neko*—kitten
> 子馬 *ko uma*—pony
> 子豚 *ko buta*—piglet [The Three Little Pigs in Japanese is 三匹の子豚 *sanbiki no kobuta*.]

Okinawa Kyushu Shikoku Chugoku **Kansai** Chubu Kanto Tohoku Hokkaido

Battle Nine: MASTER KUMA'S CHALLENGE

THE SHINKANSEN, BULLET TRAIN, MAKES TRAVELING JAPAN EASY, QUICK, BUT EXPENSIVE.

ACROSS

4 eye
5 sheep
7 pig
8 ear
11 face
12 tooth
13 mouth
15 chin
16 horse
17 lion

DOWN

1 lips
2 mouse
3 goat
6 panda
9 tiger
10 tongue
11 giraffe
12 nose
14 elephant

Okinawa Kyushu Shikoku Chugoku **Kansai** Chubu Kanto Tohoku Hokkaido

20.　Wakayama 和歌山

Japanese: 和歌山県 *wakayama ken*
Capital: 和歌山 Wakayama
Population: 989,983 (April 1, 2012)

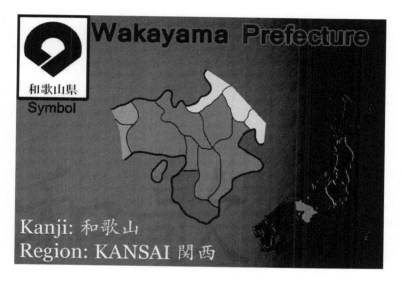

DID YOU KNOW?

Wakayama has ten World Heritage Sites for its many temples and shrines. It is near Osaka, Kyoto, and Nara, but it has many off-the-beaten paths often overlooked by tourists.

Places to See:

- **Wakayama Castle**—originally built in 1585, it was destroyed during World War II. The current reconstruction was completed in 1958.
- **Nachi Falls**—one of the best known waterfalls in Japan with a drop of 133 meters (436 feet).

Famous for:

- **Mikan**—delicious, easy-to-peel oranges.
- **Umeboshi**—salty-sour pickled plums.
- **Shichi River Dam** in Kozagawa is famous for its cherry blossoms.
- **Morihei Ueshiba** who founded the martial art, Aikido, was from Wakayama.

Vocabulary Lesson 20: Weather

天気 *tenki* weather

晴れ *hare* sunny

曇り *kumori* cloudy

雷 *kaminari* thunder

風 *kaze* wind

雨 *ame* rain

雪 *yuki* snow

台風 *taifuu* typhoon

傘 *kasa* umbrella

蒸し暑い *mushi atsui* humid

Some useful expressions include:

> いい天気ですね。 *ii tenki desu ne.* It is nice weather, isn't it?
>
> 風が強いです。 *kaze ga tsuyoi desu.* The wind is blowing hard.
>
> 雪が降りそうです。 *yuki ga furisou desu.* It looks like it will snow.
>
> 台風がきます。 *taifuu ga kimasu.* A typhoon is coming.

The difference between a typhoon and hurricane is simply its location. Japan has typhoons; America has hurricanes.

21. Nara 奈良

Japanese: 奈良県 *nara ken*
Capital: 奈良 Nara
Population: 1,396,849 (March 1, 2011)

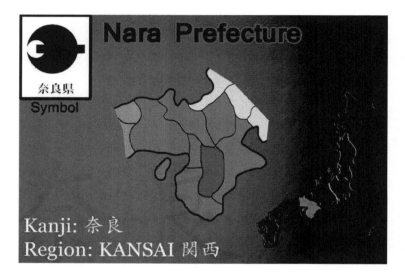

DID YOU KNOW?

Over 1,300 years old, Nara was the first permanent capital of Japan.

Places to See:

- **Horyuji Temple**—the world's oldest surviving wooden structure at over 1,300 years old.
- **Mount Yoshino** has around 30,000 cherry blossom trees.
- **Koriyama Castle**—built in 1580, but today only ruins remain. It is surrounded by gardens and cherry blossom trees.
- **Heijo Palace**—the imperial palace during the Nara Period (710 AD-794) when Nara was the capital of Japan.
- **Nara Park**—a large public park and the best place to see deer.

Famous for:

- **Deer**—wild sika deer wander around freely especially in Nara Park.
- **Kaki persimmon.**
- Well known for manufacturing **brush and ink** for Japanese calligraphy and wooden or bamboo instruments for use in the tea ceremony.
- Nara sports many, many **ancient temples and shrines.**
- **Daibutsuden**—houses the world's largest bronze statue of the Buddha.

Okinawa Kyushu Shikoku Chugoku **Kansai** Chubu Kanto Tohoku Hokkaido

- **Shousouin**—the treasure house with artifacts from Emperor Shoumu (701-756 AD) and Empress Koumyou (701-760).

 Vocabulary Lesson 21: Emergency

助けて！ *tasukete!* Help!

危ない！ *abunai!* Danger!

警察 *keisatsu* police

火事 *kaji* fire

地震 *jishin* earthquake

救急車 *kyuukyuusha* ambulance

消防車 *shoubousha* fire engine

病院 *byouin* hospital

病気 *byouki* sick

けが *kega* injury

In Japan, the emergency phone number is almost opposite to that of the United States.

- 119 dials ambulance or fire rescue.
- 110 dials the police.

Battle Ten: MASTER NEKO'S CHALLENGE

THE KANSAI REGION IS FAMOUS FOR ITS MANZAI, A TRADITIONAL STYLE OF STAND-UP COMEDY.

ACROSS

3 ambulance
7 cloudy
8 rain
9 fire engine
10 weather
12 earthquake
13 thunder
14 sick

DOWN

1 snow
2 sunny
4 police
5 umbrella
6 hospital
10 typhoon
11 fire
13 wind

Okinawa Kyushu Shikoku Chugoku **Kansai** Chubu Kanto Tohoku Hokkaido

22.　Kyoto 京都

Japanese: 京都府 *kyouto fu*
Capital: 京都 Kyoto
Population: 2,633,428 (March 1, 2011)

DID YOU KNOW?

For over 1,000 years, Kyoto was the capital of Japan. Even when the emperor was powerless, Kyoto was the imperial capital of Japan until Tokugawa Ieyasu moved the capital to Edo (present day Tokyo). The Emperor moved to Tokyo in 1868.

Places to See:

- **Kinkakuji**—the Golden Pavilion is the iconic image of Kyoto. It is covered in gold leaf and surrounded by beautiful gardens.
- **Nijo Castle**—the location the last shogun handed over power to the emperor in 1867. The Nightingale floors are so called because they "chirp" when stepped on, alerting the guards of intruders.
- **Kyoto Imperial Palace**—the residence of the imperial family until 1868.
- **Higashiyama**—a district preserved to enjoy traditional old Kyoto.
- **Gion**—Kyoto's famous geisha district.
- **Arashiyama**—the name of a mountain and district on the western outskirts of Kyoto, known for its scenic beauty.

Famous for:

- **Tourism**—Kyoto's economy depends on tourism.
- **Nintendo** is headquartered in Kyoto City.
- The city of Kyoto is still **Japan's cultural capital.**
- **Annual festivals** from ancient times: Aoi Matsuri (started 544 AD), Gion Matsuri (started 869 AD), Daimonji Gozan Okuribi (started 1662 AD).
- Kyoto prefecture has **1,600 Buddhist temples and 400 Shinto shrines.**

Okinawa Kyushu Shikoku Chugoku **Kansai** Chubu Kanto Tohoku Hokkaido

- **Kiyomizu-yaki**—porcelain with penetrating blue, yellow, and green colors and refined designs.
- **Kyoto Station**—the second largest train station in Japan with department stores, a shopping mall, a frightfully tall escalator, and more, under one 15-story roof.

 Vocabulary Lesson 22: Food

食べ物 *tabemono* food
食べる *taberu* to eat
肉 *niku* meat
ご飯 *gohan* rice (cooked)
寿司 *sushi* sushi
てんぷら *tempura* tempura
ラーメン *ra-men* ramen (noodles)
味噌汁 *miso shiru* miso soup
カレーライス *kare raisu* curry and rice
ハンバーガー *hamba-ga-* hamburger
弁当 *bentou* a lunch (box)

With rice being a staple, the word "*gohan*" itself means meal.

- 朝ご飯 *asa gohan*—breakfast
- 昼ご飯 *hiru gohan*—lunch
- 晩ご飯 *ban gohan*—supper

23.   Mie 三重

Japanese: 三重県 *mie ken*
Capital: 津 Tsu
Population: 1,855,177 (April 1, 2010)

DID YOU KNOW?

Ise Ninjutsu, a major school of ninjutsu, was based in Mie.

Okinawa Kyushu Shikoku Chugoku **Kansai** Chubu Kanto Tohoku Hokkaido

Places to See:

- **Ninja Museum**—dedicated to the history of ninja and ninjutsu.
- **Ise Shrine complex**—ancient Shinto shrines surrounded by dense forest and gravel paths.
- **Edo Wonderland**—a theme park in the style of a small castle town when the samurai ruled the country.
- **Toba Aquarium**—a large aquarium.

Famous for:

- **Traditional handicrafts** such as pottery, braiding, ink, and dyeing fabrics.
- **Mikan**—mandarin oranges that are easy to peel with fingers.
- Iga City is the birthplace of the most famous haiku poet **Matsuo Basho** as well as the **Iga style of ninjutsu.**
- **Akafuku**—a sweet made with mochi and azuki beans (sweet red bean paste).
- **Matsusaka Beef**—high ratio fat-to-meet beef from black-haired cattle from the Matsusaka region of Mie.
- **Ise Grand Shrine**—supposedly, the ancient *Yata no Kagami,* or sacred mirror from ancient times, resides here.

Vocabulary Lesson 23: Birds

ニワトリ *niwatori* chicken
鶴 *tsuru* crane (bird)
ペンギン *pengin* penguin
鷲 *washi* eagle
鳩 *hato* pigeon; dove
カラス *karasu* crow
ツバメ *tsubame* swallow
アヒル *ahiru* duck
ペリカン *perikan* pelican
キツツキ *kitsutsuki* woodpecker

カラス *karasu* or Japanese crows are huge compared to the American varieties. They are very intelligent and have made themselves at home in many Japanese cities. From stealing food to getting into uncovered trashbags, crows can be a major nuisance.

The sound they make in Japanese is カーカー *ka-ka-*.

For the most part, Japanese doesn't distinguish between "pigeon" or "dove" with 鳩 *hato*. Pigeons are seemingly everywhere in the cities of Japan.

Okinawa Kyushu Shikoku Chugoku **Kansai** Chubu Kanto Tohoku Hokkaido

Battle Eleven: MASTER PANDA'S CHALLENGE

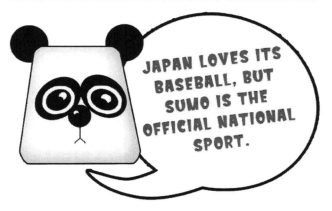

JAPAN LOVES ITS BASEBALL, BUT SUMO IS THE OFFICIAL NATIONAL SPORT.

ACROSS

5 eagle
6 penguin
8 food
9 meat
11 sushi
13 tempura
14 duck

DOWN

1 rice (cooked)
2 ramen (noodles)
3 miso soup
4 a lunch (box)
7 chicken
10 crow
12 pigeon

Okinawa Kyushu Shikoku Chugoku **Kansai** Chubu Kanto Tohoku Hokkaido

忍者
ペンギン
ninja penguin

24. Shiga 滋賀

Japanese: 滋賀県 *shiga ken*
Capital: 大津 Otsu
Population: 1,402,132 (August 1, 2009)

DID YOU KNOW?

Lake Biwa, Japan's largest lake, is at the heart of Shiga prefecture. Otsu, the capital of Shiga, was also the capital of Japan briefly from 667 to 672.

Places to See:

- **Hikone Castle**—a very well preserved Edo period castle and one of only twelve Japanese castles with the original keep.
- **Lake Biwa**—the largest lake in Japan.
- **Nagahama Castle**—originally built in 1576, the castle was soon demolished and its materials used to build the Hikone Castle. The Nagahama Castle that stands today is a 1983 reconstruction.
- **Nagahama Railway Square**—a railway museum exhibiting the history of the Nagahama Station—the oldest rail station in Japan.
- **Ho Koen**—a beautiful garden near the reconstructed Nagahama Castle. It is famous for its cherry blossoms.

Famous for:

- **Lake Biwa**—the largest lake in Japan.
- **Ninja Village** and Koka City (also known in the past as Koga City), the home for the **Koga ninja clan**, fierce rivals of the nearby Iga ninjas in Mie prefecture.
- **Omi beef** from the town Ryuo.
- **Funa-zushi**—an ancient style of sushi with a strong odor.
- Parts of **The Tale of Genji**, the world's oldest novel by Lady Murasaki, may have been written in Shiga.
- **Shigaraki-yaki**—pottery often representing tanuki, the Japanese raccoon dog.

Okinawa Kyushu Shikoku Chugoku **Kansai** Chubu Kanto Tohoku Hokkaido

Okinawa Kyushu Shikoku Chugoku **Kansai** Chubu Kanto Tohoku Hokkaido

 Vocabulary Lesson 24: Days of the Week

日曜日 *nichiyoubi* Sunday

月曜日 *getsuyoubi* Monday

火曜日 *kayoubi* Tuesday

水曜日 *suiyoubi* Wednesday

木曜日 *mokuyoubi* Thursday

金曜日 *kinyoubi* Friday

土曜日 *doyoubi* Saturday

週 *shuu* a week

先週 *sen shuu* last week

今週 *kon shuu* this week

来週 *rai shuu* next week

Like most languages, the names of the days of the week are based on planetary names or an elemental force of nature:

日 *nichi*—the sun

月 *getsu*—the moon

火 *ka*—fire

水 *sui*—water

木 *moku*—wood

金 *kin*—gold

土 *do*—the earth; ground

25. Gifu 岐阜

Japanese: 岐阜県 *gifu ken*
Capital: 岐阜 Gifu
Population: 2,074,158 (August 1, 2011)

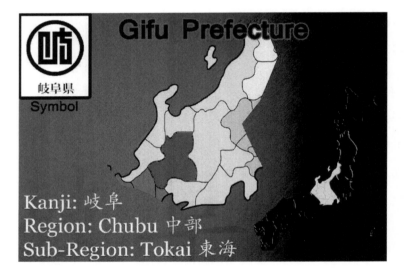

Symbol: 岐阜県

Kanji: 岐阜
Region: Chubu 中部
Sub-Region: Tokai 東海

DID YOU KNOW?

Right in the heart of Japan, Gifu has been Japan's crossroads between the east and the west. Many decisive battles took place in Gifu including Sekigahara, which was the battle that led to Tokugawa Ieyasu consolidating his power.

Places to See:

- **Takayama**—often referred to as Little Kyoto for its old buildings and historical charm.
- **Gifu Castle**—a beautiful modern reconstruction of a 13th century Japanese castle atop Mt. Kinka. Oda Nobunaga resided here for a while.
- **Shirakawago**—a historic village surrounded by mountains. The houses have steep thatched roofs and have been maintained in the traditional construction. The houses are built to withstand heavy snow. As the snow builds, the higher floors become the front door.

A Traditional Thatched-roof House in Shirakawa, Gifu
[photo from Wikipedia]

Okinawa Kyushu Shikoku Chugoku Kansai **Chubu** Kanto Tohoku Hokkaido

Famous for:

- The site of the **Battle of Sekigahara** which led to the beginning of the Edo period.
- According to the 2005 Japanese census, **the center of population in Japan** is located in Seki, Gifu.
- Historically famous for **swordmaking.** The city of Seki was renowned for the best swords in Japan.
- Gifu was so named in 1567 by **Oda Nobunaga** who was the first of three daimyo to unify Japan under the shogunate (his successors were Toyotomi Hideyoshi and Tokugawa Ieyasu).
- **Papermaking**—particularly, *Mino washi*, which is stronger and thinner than most other Japanese papers.
- Paper-based products such as **Gifu Lanterns** and **Gifu Umbrellas.**
- **Aerospace engineering** (Kakamigahara Aerospace Science Museum).
- **Nagara River**—one of the "Three Clear-Flowing Rivers in Japan" and a top tourist destination for bathers and onsen seekers.

岐阜

Vocabulary Lesson 25: Fruit

果物 *kudamono* fruit

リンゴ *ringo* apple

桃 *momo* peach

苺 *ichigo* strawberry

梨 *nashi* pear

オレンジ *orenji* orange

レモン *remon* lemon

さくらんぼ *sakuranbo* cherry

梅 *ume* plum

バナナ *banana* banana

西瓜 *suika* watermelon

The *Nashi* or Japanese Pear is more rounded like an apple than "pear-shaped." The *Kaki* or Japanese persimmon is much larger than the persimmon variety found in the States. And a traditional winter snack involves eating *Mikan* (Mandarin orange that is very easy to peel with one's fingers) while reclining under a *kotatsu*. A *kotatsu* is a heated table with a heavy blanket draped over it—an absolute pleasure in the cold winter months.

Battle Twelve: MASTER KUMA'S CHALLENGE

ACROSS

1 pear
2 Wednesday
6 this week
7 Saturday
9 plum
10 peach
12 Tuesday
13 apple
16 next week
17 cherry
18 orange

DOWN

1 Sunday
2 last week
3 strawberry
4 fruit
5 Monday
6 Friday
8 watermelon
11 Thursday
14 a week
15 banana
16 lemon

26. Fukui 福井

Japanese: 福井県 *fukui ken*
Capital: 福井 Fukui
Population: 803,755 (April 1, 2011)

Fukui Prefecture

福井県
Symbol

Kanji: 福井
Region: Chubu 中部
Sub-Region: Hokuriku 北陸

DID YOU KNOW?

Set on the Sea of Japan, Fukui became a prefecture in 1871, the majority of it formerly being called Echizen. While a small prefecture population-wise, Fukui boasts of having a world-class Dinosaur Museum—the only one in all of Japan, a town (Sabae) that produces 90% of Japan's eyeglasses, and several nuclear power plants that power about half of the Kansai regional power needs.

Places to See:

- **Ichijōdani Asakura Family Historic Ruins**—an important archeological park of an area controlled by the Asakura clan during the Sengoku period. Oda Nobunaga defeated the Asakura family and burned the town down in 1573. Much of the town has been restored and is open to the public.
- **Maruoka Castle**—built in 1576, Maruoka Castle has the oldest still-standing keep in Japan.
- **Fukui Dinosaur Museum**—a world-class museum.
- **Fukui Castle/prefectural government offices**—while the government offices are built on the ruins of Fukui Castle, the moat and original walls make it a place to visit.
- **Tōjinbō**—an area of unique sea-side rock formations.

Famous for:

- **Eyeglasses**—90% of Japan's domestically-made glasses are made in Sabae.
- **Papermaking**—Washi no Sato has museums and places to experience traditionally made paper.
- **Echizen Crab.**
- **Power**—has fourteen nuclear reactors, more than any other prefecture. These supply about half of the Kansai Region's needs.
- **Dinosaurs**—many dinosaur fossils have been found in Fukui.

Vocabulary Lesson 26: Family

FAMILY WORDS *in Japanese*

家族 *kazoku* family

お父さん *otousan* father

お母さん *okaasan* mother

息子 *musuko* son

娘 *musume* daughter

兄 *ani* older brother

弟 *otouto* younger brother

姉 *ane* older sister

妹 *imouto* younger sister

赤ちゃん *akachan* baby

The above lists the most common and useful terms of family relationships. However, it should be noted that there are different words used whether you are talking about your own family or talking about someone else's family. Japanese also distinguishes between older and younger siblings.

See **Appendix A** for a full chart.

27. Ishikawa 石川

Japanese: 石川県 *ishikawa ken*
Capital: 金沢 Kanazawa
Population: 1,168,929 (February 1, 2011)

Ishikawa Prefecture

石川県
Symbol

Kanji: 石川
Region: Chubu 中部
Sub-Region: Hokuriku 北陸

DID YOU KNOW?

Ishikawa prefecture has a mostly mountainous south, a narrow peninsula to the north, and a few islands. Kanazawa, its capital, has a metropolitan feel while richly preserving a traditional Japan of the past.

Places to See:

- **Kenrokuen**—one of Japan's three best gardens.
- **1000 Rice Fields**—**Senmaida**, found on the Noto Peninsula is a hillside with over a thousand rice fields.

- **Chaya district**—go back in time to enjoy traditional wooden houses and performances by geisha.
- With all its traditional crafts, Kanazawa is a great place to buy **unique Japanese gifts and souvenirs.**

Famous for:

- **Traditional Japanese culture**—geisha, traditional art and crafts, old wooden buildings.
- **Kanazawa lacquerware**—high quality lacquerware decorated with gold dust.
- **Kanazawa gold leaf**—traditional craft of beating gold into ultra-thin sheets called *kinpaku*.
- **Wagashi**—famous for traditional candies still made the old fashioned way.

Okinawa Kyushu Shikoku Chugoku Kansai **Chubu** Kanto Tohoku Hokkaido

111

Vocabulary Lesson 27: Counting Days

一日 *tsuitachi* 1st of the month
二日 *futsuka* 2nd of the month; 2 days
三日 *mikka* 3rd of the month; 3 days
四日 *yokka* 4th of the month; 4 days
五日 *itsuka* 5th of the month; 5 days
六日 *muika* 6th of the month; 6 days
七日 *nanoka* 7th of the month; 7 days
八日 *youka* 8th of the month; 8 days
九日 *kokonoka* 9th of the month; 9 days
十日 *tooka* 10th of the month; 10 days
二十日 *hatsuka* 20th of the month; 20 days

If you learn the above, you can easily come up with the rest of the days of the month. Simply use the "Chinese" numbers with *nichi*. For example, the 11th is *juuichi nichi*.

To say a span of days—two days time, for example—simply add "*kan*" after the name of the day. EXCEPT—isn't there always an exception?—one day. To say "one day," use *ichi nichi*.

1 day = 一日 *ichi nichi*
2 days = 二日間 *futsuka kan*
10 days = 十日間 *tooka kan*
25 days = 二十五日間 *nijuugo nichi kan*

Many Japanese make good use of the very convenient train system and flood popular tourist traps like Kanazawa's Kenrokuen. The "obvious" tourist with his camera and fanny pack may simply be someone from the next prefecture over.

28. Toyama 富山

Japanese: 富山県 *toyama ken*
Capital: 富山 Toyama
Population: 1,104,239 (February 1, 2008)

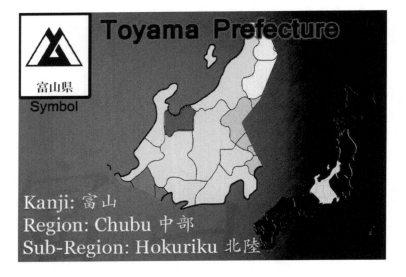

富山県
Symbol

Toyama Prefecture

Kanji: 富山
Region: Chubu 中部
Sub-Region: Hokuriku 北陸

DID YOU KNOW?

With the massive Northern Alps and heavy winter snow, the penguin is starting to feel right at home. The prefectural symbol depicts the Tateyama Mountain Range and includes a stylized hiragana と in black in the center.

In 1582 Kenshin Uesugi's 4,000 soldiers met Oda Nobunaga's army of 40,000 around Uozu Castle. Uesugi lost, but Nobunaga was soon assassinated.

Places to See:

- **The Tateyama Kurobe Alpine Route**—a spectacular route through the Northern Japan Alps via buses, cable cars, and a ropeway.
- **Kurobe Gorge**—a forested ravine in the Northern Japan Alps. Take a scenic railway through the winding paths for a spectacular view.
- **Gokayama**—similar to Shirakawago in Gifu, Gokayama is a small group of villages that have maintained their steeply pitched thatched roofs. Many houses are over 300 years old.
- **Toyama Folk Village**—a series of cultural museums in original houses.
- **Uozu Aquarium**—a large aquarium founded in 1913.

Famous for:

- High quality **rice**.
- **Pharmaceutical industry.**
- **Kurobe Dam**—at 186 meters (610 feet), it is Japan's tallest dam.
- The creator of the beloved children's character **Doraemon, Fujiko Fujio**, was born in Toyama.
- **Tulips**—Toyama is well known for its tulips including many tourist events and fairs.
- **Uozu's Three Mysteries**—a mirage over Toyama Bay, the firefly squid that emits light from their bodies, and the buried forest of underwater ceders.

Okinawa Kyushu Shikoku Chugoku Kansai **Chubu** Kanto Tohoku Hokkaido

Vocabulary Lesson 28: Times and Seasons

日 *hi* a day

今日 *kyou* today

昨日 *kinou* yesterday

明日 *ashita* tomorrow [also: あす *asu*]

年 *nen* a year [also とし *toshi*]

去年 *kyonen* last year

今年 *kotoshi* this year

来年 *rainen* next year

春 *haru* spring

夏 *natsu* summer

秋 *aki* fall; autumn

冬 *fuyu* winter

There are many helpful prefixes in Japanese that will substantially increase your vocabulary with minimal effort. One such prefix is 今 which by itself means "now." Its pronunciation is somewhat irregular, but learn these well:

今日 *kyou*—today; 今週 *konshuu*—this week; 今月 *kongetsu*—this month; 今年 *kotoshi*—this year

Another is 来 *rai* meaning "to come."

来週 *raishuu*—next week; 来月 *raigetsu*—next month; 来年 *rainen*—next year

Battle Thirteen: MASTER TANUKI'S CHALLENGE

ACROSS

- **2** today
- **6** younger sister
- **7** fall; autumn
- **11** last year
- **13** summer
- **14** family
- **16** daughter
- **18** this year
- **19** older sister
- **20** baby

DOWN

- **1** winter
- **2** yesterday
- **3** mother
- **4** older brother
- **5** next year
- **8** spring
- **9** a year
- **10** younger brother
- **12** father
- **15** tomorrow
- **17** son
- **21** a day

29. Aichi 愛知

Japanese: 愛知県 *aichi ken*
Capital: 名古屋 Nagoya
Population: 7,408,640 (February 1, 2011)

DID YOU KNOW?

A densely populated prefecture with Toyota headquartered in its namesake city, Toyota City. Nagoya is Japan's fourth largest city. The prefectural symbol depicts the rising sun over the waves while also being a stylized あいち, the hiragana for Aichi.

Places to See:

- Tour of the **Toyota car factory** in the city of Toyota.
- **Port of Nagoya Public Aquarium**—a large aquarium.
- **The four castles** in Nagoya, Okazaki, Toyohashi, and Inuyama.
- **Meiji Village** is an open-air museum exhibiting the architecture of the Meiji period (1868-1912).
- **Kourankei**—a beautiful valley located in eastern Toyota City. It is famous for having over 4,000 momiji (maple) trees. A must see in the fall when the leaves change colors.

 Famous for:

- **The three unifiers: Oda Nobunaga, Toyotomi Hideyoshi, and Tokugawa Ieyasu** were all born in what is now Aichi prefecture.
- Home of **Toyota, Brother, Noritake, Makita**, and many other large corporations.
- **Inuyama Castle**—perhaps the oldest still standing castle, dating back to 1440. Most of the castle is in its original condition.
- **Nagoya Station**—the world's largest train station.

Okinawa Kyushu Shikoku Chugoku Kansai **Chubu** Kanto Tohoku Hokkaido

Vocabulary Lesson 29: Common Expressions

なるほど *naruhodo* I see!

ちょっと待って *chotto matte* wait a little

下さい *kudasai* please

すごい *sugoi* cool!

もちろん *mochiron* Of course

例えば *tatoeba* for example

おめでとう *omedetou* congratulations

頑張って *ganbatte* You can do it!; hang in there!

大丈夫 *daijoubu* okay

本当に？ *hontou ni?* Really?

嘘 *uso* No way! [Literally, "lie."]

残念 *zannen* too bad

The above list includes some of the most useful everyday words in Japanese. In speech, you will constantly hear *naruhodo, sugoi, mochiron, daijoubu,* and *uso!*

Perhaps the most used word in Japan is *ganbaru* and its forms. It means something like "to stand firm," but it is used for encouragement, like saying "good luck."

頑張って *ganbatte*—do your best

頑張ります *ganbarimasu*—(I'll) do my best

頑張りました *ganbarimashita*—(I or you) did my best.

(vertical text, left margin) Okinawa Kyushu Shikoku Chugoku Kansai Chubu Kanto Tohoku Hokkaido

30. Shizuoka 静岡

Japanese: 静岡県 *shizuoka ken*
Capital: 静岡 Shizuoka
Population: 3,774,471 (July 1, 2010)

DID YOU KNOW?

Shizuoka was the area Tokugawa Ieyasu controlled until he conquered much of the Kanto region (present day Tokyo and surrounding area). Mt. Fuji shares a border with Shizuoka and Yamanashi prefectures.

Places to See:

- **Mt. Fuji**—officially open for climbing during July and August. The volcano is free from snow and transportation and support huts are open to the public during those months.
- **Izu Peninsula**—a resort area full of hot springs, beaches, and a clear view of Mt. Fuji.
- **Sumpu Castle**—the retirement home of Tokugawa Ieyasu. Built in 1585, it was dismantled during the Meiji Restoration. Today, the area is mostly park grounds, but the castle is being reconstructed.
- **Fuji Speedway**—an international race track where the Japanese F1 is held.
- **Atami Castle**—a 1959 concrete reconstruction, Atami Castle has a spectacular view of the city of Atami and about 200 cherry blossom trees.

Famous for:

- **Mt. Fuji**—straddling the borders of Shizuoka and Yamanashi prefectures, Fuji-san is the most iconic image of Japan. It is a volcano and talk of it erupting soon is often heard. The last major eruption was in 1707. It stands 3,776.24 meters (12,389 feet).
- **Tea**—Shizuoka accounts for 45% of Japan's overall tea production.
- Home to **Honda Motor Company, Kawai Pianos, Yamaha, Sony**, and **Suzuki Motor Company**.

- **Tokugawa Ieyasu** retired in Shizuoka and was originally buried at Kunōzan Tōshō-gū (later moved to Nikko in Tochigi prefecture).

 Vocabulary Lesson 30: Time of Day

今 *ima* now
昔 *mukashi* a long time ago
最近 *saikin* recently
朝 *asa* morning
昼 *hiru* midday
夕方 *yuugata* late afternoon
晩 *ban* evening
夜 *yoru* nighttime
すぐ *sugu* very soon
分 *fun* minute
時 *ji* hour

You can combine *ima* with *sugu* for more urgency: 今すぐ *ima sugu*—immediately.

"Food" is ご飯 *gohan*. Add time to get the names of meals:

朝ご飯 *asa gohan*—breakfast
昼ご飯 *hiru gohan*—lunch
晩ご飯 *ban gohan*—dinner

Battle Fourteen: MASTER PANDA'S CHALLENGE

ACROSS

2 minute
3 for example
5 Of course
7 too bad
11 okay
14 evening
15 now
16 late afternoon
17 very soon
19 recently
20 hour

DOWN

1 a long time ago
4 morning
6 congratulations
8 You can do it!
9 please
10 nighttime
12 midday
13 cool!
18 No way! [Literally, "lie."]

Okinawa Kyushu Shikoku Chugoku Kansai **Chubu** Kanto Tohoku Hokkaido

124

31.   Yamanashi 山梨

Japanese: 山梨県 *yamanashi ken*
Capital: 甲府 Kōfu
Population: 861,431 (February 1, 2011)

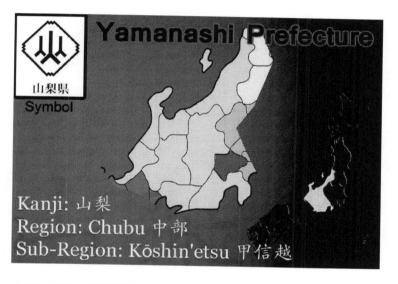

DID YOU KNOW?

The inland prefecture Yamanashi means "mountain pear" and Mt. Fuji borders Yamanashi and Shizuoka prefectures.

Okinawa Kyushu Shikoku Chugoku Kansai **Chubu** Kanto Tohoku Hokkaido

Places to See:

- **Mt. Fuji**—the northern half is in Yamanashi prefecture.
- **The Fuji Five Lakes Region**—located at the foot of Mt. Fuji, this is a great place for hiking, camping, and fishing, as well as viewing Mt. Fuji.
- **Fuji-Q Highland**—a major amusement park near Mt. Fuji. It is famous for its roller coasters, anime-themed rides, and Thomas Land, a children's area with a Thomas the Tank Engine theme.
- **Shosenkyo Gorge**—a beautiful gorge found in the Chichibu Tama Kai National Park. It is particularly spectacular during the autumn when the leaves change color.

Famous for:

- **Robotics industry.**
- **Major fruit producer** in Japan (grapes, peaches, plums).
- About 40% of the **mineral water** bottled in Japan comes from Yamanashi, taken from the Southern Alps and Mt. Fuji.
- **Koshu Wine**—the more than 80 wineries in Katsunuma produce about **40% of Japan's domestic wine.**
- **Takeda Shingen**—the famous feudal warlord was born in the area now called Yamanashi.

Vocabulary Lesson 31: Things for Eating

箸 *hashi* chopsticks

ナイフ *naifu* knife

フォーク *fouku* fork

スプーン *supuun* spoon

皿 *sara* plate

茶碗 *chawan* ricebowl

コップ *coppu* cup

丼 *donburi* a bigger bowl; a rice dish

テーブル *te-buru* table

椅子 *isu* chair

"*Donburi*" literally means a large bowl, but it is commonly used to refer to a dish consisting of rice, fish, meat, or vegetables.

32. Nagano 長野

Japanese: 長野県 *nagano ken*
Capital: 長野 Nagano
Population: 2,148,425 (February 1, 2011)

DID YOU KNOW?

Nagano was host to the 1998 Winter Olympics and borders more prefectures than any other prefecture in Japan.

Places to See:

- **Matsumoto Castle**—one of Japan's most beautiful and original castles. It was originally built from 1592 to 1614. It has the oldest five-storied wooden *donjon* (castle keep) in the country.
- **Jigokudani Wild Monkey Park**—see wild monkeys bathe in an onsen.
- **Tsumago-juku**—a town preserved to look much as it did during the feudal Edo Period.
- **Kamikochi**—a resort in the Northern Japan Alps sporting beautiful mountain scenery. It is closed in the winter.
- **Kiso Valley**—an area that was once an important trade route. The buildings have been preserved to look and feel as they did in the Edo period.
- **Karuizawa**—an often pricy mountain resort near the active volcano Mt. Asama. It is a wonderful retreat from heat of the summer.

Famous for:

- **The world-class ski resorts** at Hakuba and Shiga Kogen.
- The many mountains make it a popular place for **mountain resorts and hot springs.**
- **Japanese Alps**—nine of the twelve **highest mountains** in Japan are in Nagono.

- Nagano has one of the world's **highest geysers in Suwa** (about 40-50 meters or 131 to 164 feet).
- **Nagano apples**—second largest producer of apples in Japan. Aomori prefecture is number one.
- **Shinano soba**—Nagano's buckwheat noodles.

 Vocabulary Lesson 32: Drinks

飲み物 *nomimono* drinks
飲む *nomu* to drink
水 *mizu* water
牛乳 *gyuunyuu* milk
ジュース *ju-su* juice
コーヒー *ko-hi-* coffee
お茶 *ocha* green tea
紅茶 *kou cha* black tea
コーラ *ko-ra* cola
氷 *koori* ice

Restaurants in Japan typically do not offer free refills of drinks. To ask if refills are free, say, "*nomihoudai desu ka?*"

Jidouhanbaiki, or vending machines with drinks typically have many types of tea, hot and cold, as well as soda.

Okinawa Kyushu Shikoku Chugoku Kansai **Chubu** Kanto Tohoku Hokkaido

Battle Fifteen: MASTER NEKO'S CHALLENGE

ACROSS

1 drinks
8 plate
9 fork
10 to drink
12 cola
14 coffee
16 black tea
18 spoon
19 table

DOWN

2 green tea
3 knife
4 ricebowl
5 milk
6 chair
7 a bigger bowl; a rice dish
11 water
13 juice
15 cup
16 ice
17 chopsticks

33. Niigata 新潟

Japanese: 新潟県 *niigata ken*
Capital: 新潟 Niigata
Population: 2,371,574 (February 1, 2011)

Kanji: 新潟
Region: Chubu 中部
Sub-Region: Kōshin'etsu 甲信越

DID YOU KNOW?

Niigata means "new lagoon." The famous 16th century *daimyo* and rival of Takeda Shingen, Uesugi Kenshin was from the Niigata area. Niigata was the first port on the Sea of Japan to be opened to foreign trade after Commodore Matthew Perry opened Japan.

Places to See:

- **Sado Island**—the sixth largest island of Japan is home to the endangered Toki bird (Japanese ibis).
- **Yuzawa**—one of Japan's largest ski resorts also known for its hot springs.
- Two Niigata castles: **Kasugayama Castle** and **Shibata Castle**—both are ruins, but Shibata Castle has an original gate and is being restored.
- **Muramatsu Park**—a park with 3,000 cherry blossom trees.

Famous for:

- **Koshihikari rice**—a highly prized type of rice.
- **Rice products**: sake, mochi, senbei, and arare; Niigata is the #1 producer of rice in Japan.
- **Tulips.**
- **Koi fish**—the ornamental and colorful carp known as koi originated in Niigata.
- **Skiing** in the winter, **swimming** at the beach in the summer, and **hot springs** all year round.
- **Fireworks**—during the Nagaoka Festival in August, about 20,000 fireworks are launched.
- **Admiral Isoroku Yamamoto**—the commander-in-chief of the Combined Fleet during WWII was from Niigata. He was in charge of the attack on Pearl Harbor and the battle of Midway.

Okinawa Kyushu Shikoku Chugoku Kansai **Chubu** Kanto Tohoku Hokkaido

Vocabulary Lesson 33: Tastes

味 *aji* taste
美味しい *oishii* delicious
甘い *amai* sweet
辛い *karai* spicy
酸っぱい *suppai* sour
苦い *nigai* bitter
熱い *atsui* hot (temperature)
冷たい *tsumetai* cold (to the touch)
濃い *koi* strong/thick (liquid)
薄い *usui* weak/watery (liquid)

All of these words except *aji* (taste) are –*i* adjective words, so named because they end with –*i* and do not require any additions when added to nouns.

おいしい食べ物 *oishii tabemono*—delicious food
冷たい水 *tsumetai mizu*—cold (to the touch) water
濃いコーヒー *koi ko-hi*—strong coffee
甘いおかしい *amai okashii*—sweet snack

34.　Kanagawa 神奈川

Japanese: 神奈川県 *kanagawa ken*
Capital: 横浜 Yokohama
Population: 9,029,996 (September 1, 2010)

神奈川県
Symbol

Kanagawa Prefecture

Kanji: 神奈川
Region: Kanto 関東

DID YOU KNOW?

As the second largest prefecture by population, Kanagawa is part of the Greater Tokyo Area.

Commodore Perry landed in Kanagawa in 1853 which led to the opening of Japanese ports to the United States. To the right is The Great Wave off Kanagawa by ukiyoe artist Katsushika Hokusai.

Places to See:

- **Kamakura**—once the political center of Japan, Kamakura houses numerous historical points of interest such as one of Japan's Great Buddhas.
- **Hakone**—with a view of Mt. Fuji, Hakone has hot springs, gardens, and Lake Ashinoko, a lake formed by Mount Hakone's last eruption 3,000 years ago.
- **Hakone Botanical Garden of Wetlands**—founded in 1976, the garden has over 1,700 varieties of plants native to Japan.
- **Yokohama**—Japan's second largest city with over three million residents.
- **Zoorasia**—a large zoo in Yokohama.
- **Hakkeijima Sea Paradise**—an aquatic amusement park and aquarium.
- **Doraemon Musuem**—houses an extensive collection of the work of Fujiko F. Fujio, the creator of Doraemon. Doraemon is a robot cat from the 22nd century.

Famous for:

- **Population**—a relatively small prefecture, but is the second most populous prefecture in Japan.
- **Metropolitan Size**—Yokohama is the second largest city in Japan.
- **Yokohama Chinatown**—the largest in Japan.

Okinawa Kyushu Shikoku Chugoku Kansai Chubu **Kanto** Tohoku Hokkaido

Vocabulary Lesson 34: Useful Adjectives

楽しい *tanoshii* fun

悲しい *kanashii* sad

素晴らしい *subarashii* wonderful

面白い *omoshiroi* interesting

きれいな *kirei na* pretty

いい *ii* good

悪い *warui* bad

かわいい *kawaii* cute

正しい *tadashii* correct

美しい *utsukushii* beautiful

These adjectives are also mostly *–i* adjectives. Can you spot the one *–na* adjective in the mix?

-na adjectives like きれいな *kirei na* (pretty) drop the *–na* when used by themselves, but the *–na* is needed when added to a noun:

あ、きれい！ *a, kirei!* Ah, how pretty!

きれいな絵。 *kirei na e.* A pretty picture.

Okinawa Kyushu Shikoku Chugoku Kansai Chubu **Kanto** Tohoku Hokkaido

Battle Sixteen: MASTER NEKO'S CHALLENGE

ACROSS

4 wonderful
7 sweet
9 beautiful
10 sour
12 strong/thick (liquid)
13 cold (to the touch)
14 pretty
17 bitter
18 fun

DOWN

1 cute
2 weak/watery (liquid)
3 correct
5 hot (temperature)
6 good
8 delicious
11 interesting
12 sad
14 spicy
15 taste
16 bad

35.   Tokyo 東京

Japanese: 東京都 *tōkyō to*
Capital: 東京 Tōkyō
Population: 13,185,502 (August 1, 2011)

DID YOU KNOW?

Tokyo is the capital of Japan and the largest metropolitan area in the world. It is the seat of the Japanese government and where the Imperial Palace is located. Tokyo is made of 23 main city wards and several other cities, towns, and islands.

Someone born in Tokyo is known as 江戸っ子 *edokko*—a child of Edo, the old name for Tokyo.

Places to See:

- **Tokyo Tower**—Tokyo's iconic 333 meter (1,092) tower. Its design is based on the Eiffel Tower in Paris.
- **Akihabara**—famous for its many electronic and *otaku* shops.
- **Tsukiji Fish Market**—Japan's largest fish market.
- **Tokyo Skytree**—at 634 meters (2,080 feet), it is the tallest building in Japan. Enjoy (or be terrified by) a 360-degree panoramic view of Tokyo from the observation deck.

Famous for:

- **Crowds**—with 13 million people, Tokyo is truly a city that never sleeps.
- **Neon Jungle**—of Shibuya and Shinjuku at night.
- **Tokugawa Ieyasu** made Edo (the old name for Tokyo) his base when he became shogun in 1603.
- **Tokyo Imperial Palace**—the main residence of the Emperor of Japan.
- **Vastness**—skyscrapers, crowded subways, and the hustle and bustle of a large metropolis.
- **Regional flavors**—Shibuya for fashionable shopping; Shinjuku for luxury hotels and the seedy Kabukicho; Chiyoda for being the seat of the government as well as having the Imperial Palace; Akihabara for electronics; and many more.

Okinawa Kyushu Shikoku Chugoku Kansai Chubu **Kanto** Tohoku Hokkaido

Vocabulary Lesson 35: Outdoor Hobbies

趣味 *shumi* hobby

野球 *yakyuu* baseball

サッカー *sakka-* soccer

水泳 *suiei* swimming

山登り *yamanobori* mountain climbing

ハイキング *haikingu* hiking

ジョギング *jogingu* jogging

写真 *shashin* photograph

スキー *suki-* skiing

スケート *suke-to* skating

釣り *tsuri* fishing

You'll notice there may be a native Japanese word for a sport or they may just use the English written in katakana. Sometimes, they have both:

- Baseball is usually 野球 *yakyuu*, but it can also be written in katakana: ベースボール *be-subo-ru*.
- Swimming is usually 水泳 *suiei*, but it can be スイミング *suimingu*.
- Photograph is most often written as 写真 *shashin*, but camera is written in katakana: カメラ *kamera*.

36.   Chiba 千葉

Japanese: 千葉県 *chiba ken*
Capital: 千葉 Chiba
Population: 6,201,046 (September 1, 2010)

DID YOU KNOW?

Chiba is a part of the Greater Tokyo Area and is home to Japan's largest industrial zone.

Places to See:

- **Tokyo Disneyland**—Disney, in Japanese and actually not in Tokyo!
- **Narita Airport**—chances are, this will be the first thing you see in Japan. Truly, a tourist trap!
- **Chiba Castle**—a modern concrete reconstruction of a 12th century castle.

Famous for:

- **Peanuts**—nearly 80% of all peanuts in Japan are from Chiba.
- **Vegetables**—carrots, cabbage, daikon radish, negi, nashi pear, tomatoes, and spinach.
- **Kikkoman**—the famous soy sauce producer is headquartered in Noda, Chiba.
- **Futomaki**—fat sushi rolls, some up to 4″ in diameter.
- **Watermelons**—Tomisato city, Chiba probably produces more watermelons than any other place in Japan.

Vocabulary Lesson 36: Around the House

本棚 *hondana* bookshelf

ベッド *beddo* bed

ソファ *sofa* sofa

電気 *denki* electric light

ドア *doa* door

窓 *mado* window

枕 *makura* pillow

布団 *futon* Japanese-style floor bedding

押入れ *oshiire* closet

畳 *tatami* tatami (straw floor)

You may have heard the term "futon" in the US referring to a fold-out couch. *Futon* in Japanese is a traditional Japanese bedding consisting of thick quilts placed on the floor. It is folded and stored during the day.

Tatami is a type of straw mat used in traditional Japanese-style rooms. Most Japanese houses have at least one Japanese-style room called "*washitsu*" with tatami and traditional decor.

Okinawa Kyushu Shikoku Chugoku Kansai Chubu **Kanto** Tohoku Hokkaido

Battle Seventeen: MASTER INU'S CHALLENGE

TOKYO DISNEYLAND IS ACTUALLY IN CHIBA PREFECTURE.

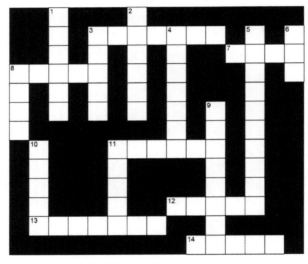

ACROSS

3 photograph
7 window
8 hobby
11 tatami (straw floor)
12 light
13 closet
14 Japanese-style floor bedding

DOWN

1 pillow
2 baseball
3 swimming
4 bookshelf
5 mountain climbing
6 door
8 sofa
9 hiking
10 bed
11 fishing

37. Saitama 埼玉

Japanese: 埼玉県 *saitama ken*
Capital: 埼玉 Saitama
Population: 7,190,817 (September 1, 2010)

DID YOU KNOW?

Saitama is a part of the Greater Tokyo Area and has seen its
population triple since 1960.

Places to See:

- **Tobu Animal Park**—a zoo, amusement park, and a pool.
- **Railway Museum**—opened in 2007, the museum showcases the history of railway in Japan.
- **Omiya Bonsai Village**—an area with several bonsai nurseries and a museum.
- **Kawagoe's Warehouse District**—sporting many *kurazukuri* clay-walled buildings, Kawagoe has a feel of an Edo Period town.

Famous for:

- **Kobaton**—a Eurasian collared dove is the prefectural mascot and prefectural bird.
- **Sayama Tea**—a type of green tea grown in the southwestern region of Saitama. The leaves are known to be thicker than most other types.
- **Bonsai Trees.**
- **Tokorozawa**—a city that was the inspiration for the anime My Neighbor Totoro.
- **Crayon Shinchan**—the popular five-year-old manga character is set in Kasukabe, Saitama.
- **Soccer**—home of the Urawa Red Diamonds and Omiya Ardija, two professional association football (soccer) teams.

Okinawa Kyushu Shikoku Chugoku Kansai Chubu **Kanto** Tohoku Hokkaido

Vocabulary Lesson 37: Indoor Hobbies

マンガ *manga* comic books
アニメ *anime* animated movies
映画 *eiga* movie
相撲 *sumou* sumo
空手 *karate* karate
柔道 *juudou* judo
剣道 *kendou* kendo
書く *kaku* to draw/write
縫う *nuu* to sew
読む *yomu* to read

Sumo is the national sport of Japan. It is also found in several other words:

指相撲 *yubi zumou*—thumb wrestling [Notice the "s" in *sumou* changes sound to a "z" when connected to another word.]
腕相撲 *ude zumou*—arm wrestling
紙相撲 *kami zumou*—paper sumo [A children's game playing sumo with paper cut-out wrestlers.]

Okinawa Kyushu Shikoku Chugoku Kansai Chubu **Kanto** Tohoku Hokkaido

38. Gunma 群馬

Japanese: 群馬県 *gunma ken*
Capital: 前橋 Maebashi
Population: 2,014,608 (March 1, 2008)

Kanji: 群馬
Region: Kanto 関東
群馬県 Symbol
Gunma Prefecture

DID YOU KNOW?

Gunma is a landlocked, mostly mountainous prefecture. It is said to be shaped like a crane (tsuru) in flight. The symbol is the first kanji in GUNma surrounded by three sets of mountains representing Mt. Haruna, Mt. Akagi, and Mt. Myogi.

150

Places to See: Din

- **Oze National Park**—a great place to hike on well-maintained trails.
- **Manza Onsen**—a hot spring resort town where you can stay and enjoy highly acidic hot springs, supposedly good for your health.
- **Takumi no Sato**—experience traditional Japanese crafts at this arts and crafts village. There are many workshops open to the public to try things such as washi paper, making soba noodles, indigo dyeing, and other traditional Japanese arts.

Famous for:

- **Horses**—the area of Gunma was an ancient center for horsebreeding.
- **Konnyaku**—produces 90% of Japanese konnyaku, a food made from the root of the konjac plant.
- **Car industry**—the Subaru factory is headquartered there.
- **Jomo Karuta**—a type of karuta card game specifically about areas and the culture of Gunma. Jomo is an old name for the area.
- **Karakkaze 空っ風**—a strong, but dry wind.
- **Melody Roads**—roads with grooves cut into them at specific intervals that when driven over at a certain speed, the grooves cause the tires to vibrate and play songs.

- **Daruma Doll**—the roly-poly toy/good luck charm originated in Takasaki City, Gunma. It is a major part of Japanese culture in words like *yukidaruma* (snow man), *Daruma Otoshi* game, and the red light/green light type of game, *Darumasan ga Koronda*.

 Vocabulary Lesson 38: Household Appliances

電子レンジ *denshi renji* microwave oven
炊飯器 *suihanki* rice cooker
洗濯機 *sentakuki* washing maching (laundry)
[This is usually pronounced *sentakki*.]
扇風機 *senpuuki* electric fan
ストーブ *suto-bu* kerosene heater
冷蔵庫 *reizouko* refrigerator
ポット *potto* hot water pot
掃除機 *soujiki* vacuum cleaner
パソコン *pasokon* PC/computer
テレビ *terebi* television

A 電気ポット *denki potto* is an electric hot water pot and is very convenient when making tea.

You may think ストーブ *suto-bu* could mean an oven/stove, but it is only used for the non-food related kerosene heaters. An oven in Japanese is オーブン *o-bun*. Ovens in Japan are often small and many are an oven/microwave oven combo.

Battle Eighteen: MASTER PANDA'S CHALLENGE

ACROSS

1 comic books
4 television
5 sumo
6 karate
10 electric fan
14 washing maching (laundry) [This is
   usually pronounced sentakki.]
15 vacuum cleaner
16 hot water pot
17 to read
18 animated movies
19 rice cooker

DOWN

2 to sew
3 movie
5 kerosene heater
7 judo
8 microwave oven
9 to draw/write
11 kendo
12 refrigerator
13 PC/computer

39. Ibaraki 茨城

Japanese: 茨城県 *ibaraki ken*
Capital: 水戸 Mito
Population: 2,964,141 (September 1, 2010)

DID YOU KNOW?

Ibaraki is the home of the martial art, Aikido, and it is the largest producer of natto (fermented soybeans). Ibaraki is growing as the Greater Tokyo Area spreads north.

Places to See:

- **Kairakuen**—one of Japan's three most celebrated gardens with over 3,000 Japanese plum trees.
- **Kodokan**—the largest school for samurai elite during the Edo Period.
- **Kamine Park and Shizumine Park**—both are famous for the cherry blossoms.

Famous for:

- **Hitachi**—founded in Hitachi City, Ibaraki.
- **Bell peppers and Chinese cabbage**—produces about a quarter of all grown in Japan.
- **Natto**—fermented (and smelly) soybeans that are said to be quite healthy.
- **Watermelons and chestnuts.**
- **Aikido**—founded by Ueshiba Morihei in Ibaraki.
- **Hoshiimo**—air-dried sweet potatoes available in the winter.

Okinawa Kyushu Shikoku Chugoku Kansai Chubu **Kanto** Tohoku Hokkaido

Vocabulary Lesson 39: Common Food

野菜 *yasai* vegetables

じゃがいも *jagaimo* potato

さつまいも *satsuma imo* sweet potato

にんじん *ninjin* carrot

たまねぎ *tamanegi* onion (round)

ねぎ *negi* green onion

トマト *tomato* tomato

牛肉 *gyuu niku* beef

チキン *chikin* chicken meat

パン *pan* bread

The "*tama*" in *tamanegi* means 玉 ball or sphere, so *tamanegi* refers to the round (normal) onions.

焼き鳥 *yakitori* or grilled chicken is probably the most common way Japanese eat chicken, but KFC is highly popular in Japan—especially for Christmas!

Natto (納豆. *nattou*) is a traditional Japanese food made from fermented soybeans. It is often eaten for breakfast over rice. It is said to be quite healthy—full of protein—but it has a powerful smell not unlike recently discarded socks sweltering in the summer sun.

Natto is often packaged in containers as shown below.

40.   Tochigi 栃木

Japanese: 栃木県 *tochigi ken*
Capital: 宇都宮 Utsunomiya
Population: 2,005,096 (November 1, 2010)

DID YOU KNOW?

The imperial family has a villa in Nasu, Tochigi. Ashikaga Gakko in Ashikaga City is the oldest higher-learning academic institution in Japan. It had its beginnings in the ninth century.

Places to See:

- **Kegon Falls**—beautiful waterfalls in Nikko.
- **Cedar Avenue of Nikko**—view 400-year-old Japanese Cedars.
- **Kanmangafuchi Abyss**—a gorge with a walking trail.
- **Nikko Botanical Garden**—owned by the University of Tokyo, this garden exhibits over 2,000 plants.
- **Tamozawa Imperial Villa**—a summer residence for the Imperial family now open to the public.
- **Tobu World Square**—a theme park with 1/25th-scale replicas of famous buildings and sites across the world. See the pyramids, the Eiffel Tower, and Versailles in one day.

Famous for:

- **Onsen**—the region Nasu is famous for onsens, sake, and ski resorts.
- **Camera lenses and X-ray equipment**—produces the majority in all of Japan.
- **Toshogu**—a lavishly decorated shrine dedicated to Tokugawa Ieyasu.
- **Gyoza**—Utsunomiya has about two hundred gyoza (Chinese dumplings) shops.

Okinawa Kyushu Shikoku Chugoku Kansai Chubu **Kanto** Tohoku Hokkaido

Vocabulary Lesson 40: School Words

学校 *gakkou* school
先生 *sensei* teacher
生徒 *seito* pupil; student
小学校 *shougakkou* elementary school
中学校 *chuugakkou* middle school; junior high
高校 *koukou* high school
大学 *daigaku* university; college
校庭 *koutei* school grounds; campus
教室 *kyoushitsu* classroom
図書室 *toshoshitsu* library
教科書 *kyoukasho* textbook

Japanese schools have 掃除時間 *souji jikan*—cleaning time. For a few minutes each morning, the students put down their pencils and shitajikis (pencil boards) and pick up their brooms.

Another term for student is 学生 *gakusei*. A library, in general, is called 図書館 *toshokan*.

160

Battle Nineteen: MASTER INU'S CHALLENGE

ACROSS

1 chicken meat
4 bread
8 onion (round)
9 green onion
11 classroom
13 school grounds; campus
15 university; college
16 textbook
18 middle school; junior high
19 school
20 school library

DOWN

2 carrot
3 potato
5 elementary school
6 sweet potato
7 teacher
10 beef
12 vegetables
13 high school
14 tomato
17 pupil; student

41. Fukushima 福島

Japanese: 福島県 *fukushima ken*
Capital: 福島 Fukushima
Population: 2,028,752 (October 10, 2010)

DID YOU KNOW?

Fukushima was one of the primary regions hit by the 2011 Great East Japan Earthquake.

It is the third largest prefecture by area (Hokkaido and Iwate are number one and two respectively).

Places to See:

- **Ouchijuku**—an Edo period post town / rest area on an old trade route. It is preserved to look as it did hundreds of years ago.
- **Oze National Park**—a great hiking spot with boardwalks over vast marshlands.
- **Aizu Wakamatsu**—a castle town with samurai museums and much local history. The castle is also known as Tsuruga Castle.
- **Spa Resort Hawaiians**—opening in 1966, this was the first theme park in Japan. Enjoy onsen, a water park, and other Hawaii-themed entertainment.

Famous for:

- **Software and electronics.**
- **Fruits**—peaches in particular.
- **Fukushima Daiichi Nuclear Power Plant**—badly damaged by the 2011 earthquake and tsunami, the plant experienced explosions, fire, and released radiation.
- **Miharu Takizakura**—a cherry blossom tree that is over 1,000 years old.

Vocabulary Lesson 41: Countries

国 *kuni* a country

日本 *nihon* Japan

カナダ *kanada* Canada

韓国 *kankoku* South Korea

中国 *chuugoku* China

イギリス *igirisu* Great Britain

オーストラリア *o-sutoraria* Australia

アメリカ *amerika* America (USA)

フランス *furansu* France

イタリア *itaria* Italy

In most cases, you just add a 人 *jin* to the country name to get "a person from that country."

アメリカ人 *amerika jin*—American
日本人 *nihon jin*—Japanese (person)
フランス人 *furansu jin*—French (person)

If the language spoken is associated with the country, add a 語 (*go*) to the country:

日本語 *nihon go*—Japanese (language)
フランス語 *furansu go*—French (language)
イタリア語 *itaria go*—Italian (language)
But 英語 *ei go*—English (language)

Okinawa Kyushu Shikoku Chugoku Kansai Chubu Kanto Tohoku Hokkaido

42.   Yamagata 山形

Japanese: 山形県 *yamagata ken*
Capital: 山形 Yamagata
Population: 1,166,309 (February 1, 2011)

DID YOU KNOW?

If you are in Yamagata in the winter, you can see the Snow Monsters of Zao. A cold Siberian jet stream freezes wet snow to fir trees and makes them look like huge, white monsters.

Places to See:

- **Yamadera**—literally, "mountain temple," this scenic temple on a sharp mountainside had its start in 860 AD. It is where Matsuo Basho wrote one of his most famous poems:

閑さや岩にしみ入蝉の声
shizukasa ya iwa ni shimiiru semi no koe
The stillness, sinking into the stones, the voice of the cicada.

- **Mt. Zao**—a volcanic mountain range with a large crater lake at the summit, hot springs, and a ski resort.
- **Kaminoyama Castle**—this is a 1982 concrete reconstruction of a 16th century castle.

Famous for:

- **Cherries and Pears**—the largest producer of both in Japan.
- **Other fruits**—grapes, apples, peaches, among others.
- **Imoni**—a potato stew made in September.

Vocabulary Lesson 42: Nature

木 *ki* tree

花 *hana* flower

草 *kusa* grass

雲 *kumo* cloud

虫 *mushi* insect

鳥 *tori* bird

動物 *doubutsu* animal

魚 *sakana* fish

恐竜 *kyouryuu* dinosaur

蛇 *hebi* snake

The loudest insect in the world (so it seems to those who have experienced them...) is the セミ *semi* or cicada. During the summer in Japan, the *semi* are out in force.

The famous haiku by Basho mentioned on the previous page is about the little critter.

Battle Twenty: MASTER KUMA'S CHALLENGE

THE GENKAN, OR ENTRANCE, IS WHERE OUTSIDE SHOES ARE REMOVED BEFORE ENTERING.

ACROSS

1 Canada
4 bird
7 cloud
10 fish
12 a country
13 tree
15 China
16 Italy
17 snake
18 France

DOWN

2 Japan
3 animal
5 Great Britain
6 America (USA)
8 flower
9 grass
11 South Korea
12 dinosaur
14 insect

43.   Miyagi 宮城

Japanese: 宮城県 *miyagi ken*
Capital: 仙台 Sendai
Population: 2,337,513 (December 1, 2010)

宮城県
Symbol

Miyagi Prefecture

Kanji: 宮城
Region: Tōhoku 東北

DID YOU KNOW?

The following famous haiku about an area in Miyagi Prefecture is believed to have been written by Matsuo Basho when he was at a loss for words:

松島や ああ松島や 松島や
matsushima ya / aa matsushima ya / matsushima ya
Matsushima! Ah, Matsushima! Matsushima!

Places to See:

- **Sendai Castle** (also known as Aoba Castle)—built in 1601, it is today being restored.
- **Matsushima Bay**—a group of pine-clad scenic islands and one of the Three Views of Japan.
- **Tashirojima**—a small island famous for a large stray cat population. There are no pet dogs and the locals feed and care for the more-populous-than-humans cats.

Famous for:

- **Manufacturing industries**—such as electronics and appliances.
- **Gyutan**—grilled cow tongue, a famous Sendai dish.
- **Sendai Tanabata Matsuri**—one of the largest and most colorful Tanabata festivals in Japan held in August.
- **Mori no Miyako**—Sendai was known as the capital of forests (森の都 *mori no miyako*) because residents planted many trees in their yards. Much of the greenery was lost during World War II, but much effort has been made to restore the greenery to the city.

Vocabulary Lesson 43: Shopping

店 *mise* shop
買い物 *kaimono* shopping
デパート *depa-to* department store
スーパー *su-pa-* supermarket
お金 *okane* money
円 *en* yen (Japanese money)
百 *hyaku* one hundred
千 *sen* one thousand
万 *man* ten thousand
本屋 *honya* book shop

Way back on page 19, you learned how to count to 99. Here are a few more words to help you count to 99,999,999! See **Appendix B** for how to do it.

If you have a *yen* for correct pronunciation, Japanese money is actually pronounced, "*en.*"

Also, notice both デパート and スーパー are shortened forms of the English words "department store" and "super market," respectively. Japanese often shortens words imported from English.

44. Iwate 岩手

Japanese: 岩手県 *iwate ken*
Capital: 盛岡 Morioka
Population: 1,330,530 (October 1, 2010)

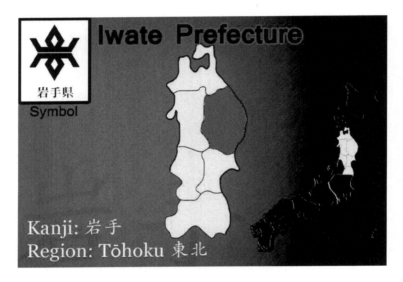

岩手県
Symbol

Iwate Prefecture

Kanji: 岩手
Region: Tōhoku 東北

DID YOU KNOW?

The second largest prefecture in area after its northern neighbor Hokkaido, Iwate literally means "rock hand."

Places to See:

- **Fujiwara no Sato**—a movie lot and theme park.
- **Tenshochi**—a park known for more than 10,000 cherry blossom trees.
- **Morioka Castle**—the ruins of which is a part of Iwate Park.
- **Geibikei**—a gorge best viewed from a calm trip on the river.
- **Ryusendo Cave**—a large limestone cave in the mountains.

 Famous for:

- **Semiconductor and communications** manufacturing.
- Costal areas were badly damaged by the **2011 earthquake.**
- **Nanbu senbei**—rice crackers.
- **Kenji Miyazawa**—the popular poet and author was born and lived in Hanamaki, Iwate. His most famous poem is *Ame ni mo makezu* which means, "be not defeated by the rain."
- **Konjiki-dou**—the "Golden Hall" is a mausoleum containing the mummified remains of leaders of the 12th century Fujiwara clan.

Okinawa Kyushu Shikoku Chugoku Kansai Chubu Kanto **Tohoku** Hokkaido

Okinawa Kyushu Shikoku Chugoku Kansai Chubu Kanto **Tohoku** Hokkaido

 ## Vocabulary Lesson 44: Relatives

親戚 *shinseki* relatives
おじいさん *ojiisan* grandfather
おばあさん *obaasan* grandmother
おばさん *obasan* aunt
おじさん *ojisan* uncle
両親 *ryoushin* parents
子供 *kodomo* children
兄弟 *kyoudai* brothers and sisters
孫 *mago* grandchild
男の子 *otoko no ko* boy
女の子 *onna no ko* girl

Notice the difference between grandfather / uncle and grandmother / aunt. The longer the vowel, the older the family member.

兄弟 *kyoudai* is generally used for brothers and sisters. However, if you are only referring to sisters, you can use 姉妹 *shimai* instead. Notice in 兄弟 the kanji are "elder brother" and "younger brother." 姉妹 are "older sister" and "younger sister."

See **Appendix A** for more on family words.

174

Battle Twenty-One: MASTER INU'S CHALLENGE

ACROSS

- **4** yen (Japanese money)
- **5** book shop
- **8** shopping
- **11** one thousand
- **13** children
- **15** supermarket
- **16** grandfather
- **17** one hundred
- **18** uncle

DOWN

- **1** ten thousand
- **2** department store
- **3** grandchild
- **6** money
- **7** shop
- **9** grandmother
- **10** brothers and sisters
- **12** parents
- **14** aunt

Okinawa Kyushu Shikoku Chugoku Kansai Chubu Kanto **Tohoku** Hokkaido

45. Akita 秋田

Japanese: 秋田県 *akita ken*
Capital: 秋田 Akita
Population: 1,106,050 (October 1, 2010)

DID YOU KNOW?

Home of both the Akita dog and the famously loyal dog named Hachiko who waited for his master every day at the Shibuya train station in Tokyo years after his master's death. A movie called *Hachi* starring Richard Gere was made about this faithful friend.

Places to See:

- **Lake Tazawa**—with many onsen resorts.
- **Kakunodate**—known as little Kyoto with its preserved samurai houses.
- **Senshu Park**—with cherry trees and a replica of Akita Castle.

Famous for:

- **Akita dog**—thought to have originated in Akita.
- **Akita bijin**—beautiful woman from Akita, reknowned for white, pure skin, round faces, and high voices.
- **Sake**—famous for sake breweries.
- **Akitakomachi**—a type of rice cross-bred from high-end rice from Fukui prefecture. Akitakomachi is a short-grain rice that is highly favored for sushi.

Okinawa Kyushu Shikoku Chugoku Kansai Chubu Kanto **Tohoku** *Hokkaido*

 Vocabulary Lesson 45: Feelings

感じ *kanji* feeling
気持ち *kimochi* mood
眠い *nemui* sleepy
疲れた *tsukareta* tired; worn-out
悲しい *kanashii* sad
嬉しい *ureshii* happy
忙しい *isogashii* busy/rushed
怖い *kowai* scary
寂しい *sabishi* lonely
ぺこぺこ *peko peko* hungry (childish)

ぺこぺこ *peko peko* is usually said to and by children:

おなかがぺこぺこ。 *onaka ga pekopeko*. I'm hungry.

Usually, adults say:

おなかがすいた。 *onaka ga suita*. I'm hungry.

Or if you want to sound rougher and more casual:

腹減った。 *hara hetta*. I'm hungry. (Masculine)

178

Gaijin (外人 *gaijin*) means "foreigner" but is often considered derogatory. It literally means "outsider." A more polite term is 外国人 *gaikokujin* which means "a person from a foreign country."

46. Aomori 青森

Japanese: 青森県 *aomori ken*
Capital: 青森 Aomori
Population: 1,373,164 (October 1, 2010)

青森県
Symbol

Aomori Prefecture

Kanji: 青森
Region: Tōhoku 東北

DID YOU KNOW?

The Seikan Tunnel links Aomori to Hokkaido. It is the longest tunnel of its kind in the world and has the second longest train tunnel.

The Aomori symbol is a stylized shape of the prefecture on a map with its three peninsulas.

Places to See:

- **Hirosaki Castle**—originally constructed in 1611, it burned down due to lightning and was not rebuilt until 1810. The surrounding castle grounds houses a beautiful park well known for its cherry blossoms.
- **Shirakami Sanchi**—a large mountain range with many hiking trails including waterfalls, ponds, and canyons.
- **Sannai Maruyama Archaeological Site**—a large Jomon Period (pre-300 BC) village museum.

Famous for:

- **Apples**—Japan's largest producer.
- **Tsugaru-jamisen**—a genre of shamisen music.
- **Aomori Nebuta Matsuri**—a Japanese summer festival in which large floats decorated with warrior illustrations are carried through the center of the city.
- **Maguro**—tuna dishes.

Vocabulary Lesson 46: Water Creatures

イルカ *iruka* dolphin

鯨 *kujira* whale

鮪 *maguro* tuna

鮫 *same* shark

イカ *ika* squid

蛸 *tako* octopus

貝 *kai* shellfish

エビ *ebi* prawn; shrimp

鯉 *koi* carp (koi)

亀 *kame* turtle

鰻 *unagi* eel

Unless you are absolutely positive you are in a Mexican restaurant (very few exist in Japan!), be careful when ordering a "*tako.*"

A trip to a traditional Japanese garden would not be complete without seeing the colorful *koi* fish. Some *koi* get quite large and they are smart enough to recognize their usual feeders. Koi normally live around 20-40 years, but one fish named Hanako supposedly lived 226 years!

182

Battle Twenty-Two:
MASTER PANDA'S CHALLENGE

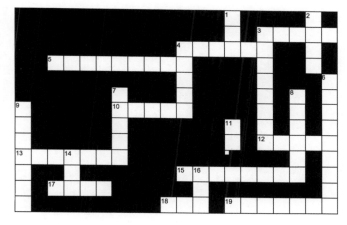

ACROSS

3 scary
4 whale
5 tired; worn-out
10 sleepy
12 dolphin
13 lonely
15 hungry (childish)
17 turtle
18 carp (koi)
19 mood

DOWN

1 shellfish
2 shark
3 sad
4 feeling
6 busy/rushed
7 eel
8 tuna
9 happy
11 octopus
14 squid
16 prawn; shrimp

47.　Hokkaido 北海道

Japanese: 北海道 *hokkaidō*
Capital: 札幌 Sapporo
Population: 5,507,456 (October 1, 2010)

DID YOU KNOW?

Like our first prefecture, Okinawa, Hokkaido is both a prefecture and a region. It is the second largest island in Japan and the most northern. It is a "*dō*" and not "*ken.*"

Places to See:

- **Sapporo**—the largest city (and capital) of Hokkaido.
- **Asahikawa**—the second largest city and officially the coldest city in Japan.
- **Matsumae Castle**—also known as Fukuyama Castle, it is famous for having over 10,000 cherry blossom trees.

Famous for:

- **Farms**—Hokkaido produces more agricultural products than any other prefecture.
- **Sapporo beer**—originally from Sapporo, Hokkaido, the world headquarters is now in Tokyo.
- **Wakkanai**—the northernmost city in Japan. The Russian island Sakhalin can be seen on a clear day.

Okinawa Kyushu Shikoku Chugoku Kansai Chubu Kanto Tohoku

Hokkaido

Okinawa Kyushu Shikoku Chugoku Kansai Chubu Kanto Tohoku

 Vocabulary Lesson 47: More Japanese Foods

和食 *wa shoku* Japanese food

洋食 *you shoku* Western food

砂糖 *satou* sugar

塩 *shio* salt

しょうゆ *shouyu* soy sauce

わさび *wasabi* wasabi (Japanese horseradish)

みそ *miso* miso paste

納豆 *nattou* natto (fermented soybeans with a strong odor)

おやつ *oyatsu* snack

豆腐 *toufu* tofu

Natto is one traditional Japanese food that is said to be quite healthy, but is also very stinky. Some Japanese do not like it, while others eat it every morning for breakfast.

味噌汁 *miso shiru* or miso soup is made from miso paste, vegetables, and tofu. Miso paste itself is made by fermenting rice, barley, or soybeans with salt and a fungus.

Hokkaido

Battle Twenty-Three:
MASTER NAMAKEMONO'S CHALLENGE

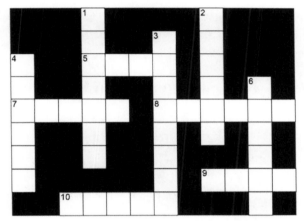

ACROSS

5 salt
7 sugar
8 soy sauce
9 miso paste
10 tofu

DOWN

1 Japanese food
2 natto (fermented soybeans with a strong odor)
3 Western food
4 wasabi (Japanese horseradish)
6 snack

Endnotes from the Penguin

I must say, for a human, you have done remarkably well. I look forward to meeting you in Japan one day. I may even let you buy me a cold one there— a very cold one, please.

The appendices have some other goodies you may wish to study. I do hope my little book has helped you in some measure.

But just remember our little secret from page one!

APPENDIX A: TERMS OF FAMILY RELATIONSHIP

Japanese has two sets of family relationship words depending on whose family member you are talking about.

	Speaking of one's own family	Speaking of another's family
Father	父 *chichi*	お父さん *otousan*
Mother	母 *haha*	お母さん *okaasan*
Husband	夫 *otto*	ご主人 *goshujin*
Wife	妻 *tsuma*	奥さん *okusan*
Grandfather	祖父 *sofu*	おじいさん *ojiisan*
Grandmother	祖母 *sobo*	おばあさん *obaasan*
Older brother	兄 *ani*	お兄さん *oniisan*
Younger brother	弟 *otouto*	弟さん *otoutosan*
Older sister	姉 *ane*	お姉さん *oneesan*
Younger sister	妹 *imouto*	妹さん *imoutosan*
Uncle	おじ *oji*	おじさん *ojisan*
Aunt	おば *oba*	おばさん *obasan*
Son	息子 *musuko*	息子さん *musukosan*
Daughter	娘 *musume*	お嬢さん *ojousan*

APPENDIX B: COUNTING IN JAPANESE

There are two sets of numbers to keep in mind when counting in Japanese: *on yomi* (pronunciations imported from Chinese) and *kun yomi* (native Japanese sounds).

For the most part, you only need to learn two sets up to ten. After that, it is regular.

	on yomi	*kun yomi*
1	*ichi*	*hitotsu*
2	*ni*	*futatsu*
3	*san*	*mittsu*
4	**yon** or *shi*	*yottsu*
5	*go*	*itsutsu*
6	*roku*	*muttsu*
7	**nana** or *shichi*	*nanatsu*
8	*hachi*	*yattsu*
9	**kyuu** or *ku*	*kokonotsu*
10	*juu*	*too*

 * 4 and 7 have two *on yomi* pronunciations. In general, the **boldfaced yon** and **nana** are used more.

The native Japanese numbers tend to only be used when counting certain things like dates—they are essential for the student to master, however.

Japanese is easier than English in that there are no special words like "twenty" or "fifty" when counting up to 99.
   To make 20, just say 2 and 10: *ni juu*.
   To make 21, say 2 – 10 – 1: *ni juu ichi*

Try to make 99 and then turn the page to find the answer.

99 is *kyuu juu kyuu.*

Numbers above 99

100 百 *hyaku*
1,000 千 *sen*
10,000 万 *man*
100,000,000 億 *oku*

The construction is exactly the same as before, just start from the left and move right:

101 is *hyaku ichi.*
1999 is *sen kyuu hyaku kyuu juu kyuu.*
20,000 is *ni man.*

APPENDIX C: KO-SO-A-DO

The demonstrative pronouns this, that, and that over there and their variants are known as こそあど *ko-so-a-do* in Japanese. This acronym tells us the function of the pronoun or word:

- こ *ko*—applies to things close to the speaker
- そ *so*—applies to things close to the listener
- あ *a*—applies to things close to neither
- ど *do*—a question word

Here are the こそあど separated by type:

Demonstrative Pronouns 〜れ
These pronouns replace a noun entirely.

- **これ *kore*—this (things close to the speaker)**
  これは何？ *kore wa nani?* What's this?
- **それ *sore*—that (things close to listener)**
  それは猫です。 *sore wa neko desu.* That is a cat.
- **あれ *are*—that over there (things close to neither)**
  あれは猫ですか？ *are wa neko desu ka?* Is that a cat over there?
- **どれ *dore*—which? (the question word)**
  どれが好きですか？ *dore ga suki desu ka?* Which do you like?

Demonstrative Adjectives ～の

These are paired with a noun to show specificity.

- **この** *kono*—**this ~ (things close to the speaker)**
  この猫は誰の？ *kono neko wa dare no?* Who's cat is this?
- **その** *sono*—**that ~ (things close to listener)**
  その猫は私のです。 *sono neko wa watashi no desu.* That cat is mine.
- **あの** *ano*—**that ~ over there (things close to neither)**
  あの猫は白いです。 *ano neko wa shiroi desu.* That cat is white.
- **どの** *dono*—**which ~? (the question word)**
  どの猫があなたのですか？ *dono neko ga anata no desu ka?* Which cat is yours?

Words that Show Location ～こ

These are pronouns that show location. They replace the noun they represent.

- **ここ** *koko*—**here (things close to speaker)**
  ここはいい場所です。 *koko wa ii basho desu.* This is a nice place.
- **そこ** *soko*—**there (things close to listener)**
  そこは穴があります。 *soko wa ana ga arimasu.* There is a hole (near you).
- **あそこ** *asoko*—**there (things close to neither)**
  あそこはいいレストランです。 *asoko wa ii resutoran desu.* That is a nice restaurant (when neither the speaker or listener is near it).
- **どこ** *doko*—**where**
  レストランはどこですか？ *resutoran wa doko desu ka?* Where is the restaurant?

Words that Show Direction ～ちら

These are pronouns that show the direction something is
moving or is generally located. They replace the noun they
represent. [The nonpolite version is in brackets.]

- こちら *kochira*—this way (things close to
  speaker) [こっち *kocchi*]
  こちらへどうぞ。 *kochira e douzo.* This way, please.
- そちら *sochira*—that way (things close to
  listener) [そっち *socchi*]
  そちらのほうが涼しい。 *sochira no hou ga suzushii.*
  That way is cooler (temperature-wise).
- あちら *achira*—that way over there (things close
  to neither) [あっち *acchi*]
  あちらは蛇がいる。 *achira wa hebi ga iru.* There is a
  snake that way over there.
- どちら *dochira*—which way? [どっち *docchi*]
  どちらに行きますか？ *dochira ni ikimasu ka?* Which
  way are you going?

Words that Show Kinds ～んな

These differentiate between kinds and they also indicate the
degree of some state or action.

- こんな *konna*—this kind of ~ (things close to the
  speaker)
  こんな車がほしいです。 *konna kuruma ga hoshii desu.* I
  want a car like this.
- そんな *sonna*—that kind of ~ (things close to
  listener)
  そんなアイデアはよくないです。 *sonna aidea wa
  yokunai desu.* Such an idea isn't good.

194

- **あんな *anna*—that kind of ~ over there (things close to neither)**
  あんな人になりたくないです。 *anna hito ni naritakunai desu.* I don't want to become a person like that.
- **どんな *donna*—which kind of ~? (the question word)**
  どんな人になりたいですか？ *donna hito ni naritai desu ka?* What kind of person do you want to be?

Words that Show a Manner of Doing 〜う
These demonstrate the manner in which something is done.

- **こう *kou*—like this (things relating to the speaker)**
  こう動いてください。 *kou ugoite kudasai.* Move like this.
- **そう *sou*—like that (things relating to listener)**
  そういうこと言わないで。 *Sou iu koto iwanaide.* Don't say things like that.
- **ああ *aa*—like that (things relating to neither)**
  ああいうデザインが好き。 *au iu dezain ga suki.* I like that kind of design.
- **どう *dou*—how? (the question word)**
  どうやってするですか？ *dou yatte suru desu ka?* How do I do it?

ANSWERS

Page 15

Page 23

Page 30

Page 37

Page 45

Page 52

Page 64

Page 74

Page 82

Page 89

Page 96

Page 106

Page 117

Page 124

Page 131

Page 138

Page 146

Page 153

Page 161

Page 168

Page 175

Page 183

Page 187

Congratulations!

For free resources to help you further your Japanese, please visit http://TheJapanesePage.com. We have many articles on kanji, grammar, and Japanese vocabulary.

FREE MP3s

To download FREE MP3s for all the example sentences found in this book, please enter this address in a browser on your computer. The filenames correspond to the numbering found in this ebook.

http://thejapanesepage.com/downloads/ninja.zip

Thank you for purchasing and reading this book! To contact the authors, please email them at *help@thejapanshop.com*. See also the wide selection of materials for learning Japanese at *www.TheJapanShop.com* and the free site for learning Japanese at *www.thejapanesepage.com*.

OTHER TITLES BY KOTOBA BOOKS
AVAILABLE IN EBOOK AND PAPERBACK

Language Instructional Books by Clay & Yumi Boutwell
www.Kotobainc.com

Hiragana, the Basics of Japanese
Japanese Reader Collection Vol 1: Hikoichi
Japanese Reader Collection Vol 2: Momotaro, the Peach Boy
Japanese Grammar 100 in Plain English
Kanji 100: Learn the Most Useful Kanji in Japanese
Kotowaza, Japanese Proverbs and Sayings

Fiction by CJ Martin
www.CJMartinBooks.com

The Temporal
A Temporal Trust
Tanaka and the Yakuza's Daughter

4690157R10113

Printed in Great Britain
by Amazon.co.uk, Ltd.,
Marston Gate.